# Differences in the Dark

# Differences

**American Movies and English Theater**

# in the Dark

*Michael T. Gilmore*

COLUMBIA UNIVERSITY PRESS

NEW YORK

COLUMBIA UNIVERSITY PRESS
Publishers Since 1893
New York    Chichester, West Sussex

Copyright © 1998 Columbia University Press
All rights reserved
Library of Congress Cataloging-in-Publication Data


Gilmore, Michael T.
   Differences in the dark  :  American movies and
   the English theater  /  Michael T. Gilmore.
      p.    cm.
   Includes bibliographical references and index.
   ISBN 0-231-11224-6 (alk. paper)
      1. Motion pictures—Social aspects—United States.
      2. Theater—Social aspects—Great Britain.    I. Title.
   PN1995.9.S6G56    1998
   302.23'43'0973—dc21                                97-50584


Casebound editions of Columbia University Press
books are printed on permanent and durable acid-free
paper.
Printed in the United States of America

c 10 9 8 7 6 5 4 3 2 1

*To Deborah, Emma, and Rosa*

# Contents

## Acknowledgments

It is a pleasure to thank the people who
helped me with this book. Because I have
strayed far outside my academic specialty
(in American literature), I have incurred
more than the usual number of debts. Peter
Weiler saved me from committing still
more blunders than I have about twentieth-
century British culture, and Steve Whitfield
performed the same generous service on
the American side. Mark Carnes was another
fount of information about American history. Gene Goodheart and Saki Bercovitch
commented with their usual penetration,
and Saki offered invaluable advice about
restructuring the argument. Jay Cantor provided encouragement when I badly needed
it and tried valiantly to bring me up to speed
on the movies. My good friend Lew Wurgaft,
an authority on imperialism, was a model
listener and critic. He made important suggestions throughout. Martin Jay, whose
mastery of intellectual history is unrivaled,
gave the manuscript a remarkably thorough reading. His wisdom, professionalism,
and kindness made a decisive difference in
improving the final product.

I also benefited from conversations
with Morton Keller (about the gold standard),
Donna Vinter and Carolyn Williams (about

English theater), Anne Janowitz (about English society), Tom King (about acting), Susan Staves (about novels and the theater), Tom Doherty (about America and the movies), Andrew Matthews (about natural resources), Jim Obelkevich (about English nature), and Leslie Epstein and Michael McKeon (about novels and the movies).

Jim Livingston gave me the chance to try out some of my ideas in public, an experience that emboldened me to turn a short essay into the longer one that has become this book. And Jennifer Crewe of Columbia University Press has been as supportive and intelligent an editor as one could hope for.

My biggest debt is to my family, for forbearance as well as love. Emma and Rosa, my two daughters, endured good plays and bad and were unfailingly forgiving about my obsession with cultural differences. My wife, Deborah Valenze, a British historian, introduced me to London in the first place. She has always been my most incisive reader. She helped me find the courage to pursue fresh directions in my work and, despite her own impatience with American popular culture, tolerated my fascination with the mainstream cinema. It is the simple truth that I could never have imagined this book, much less written it, without her.

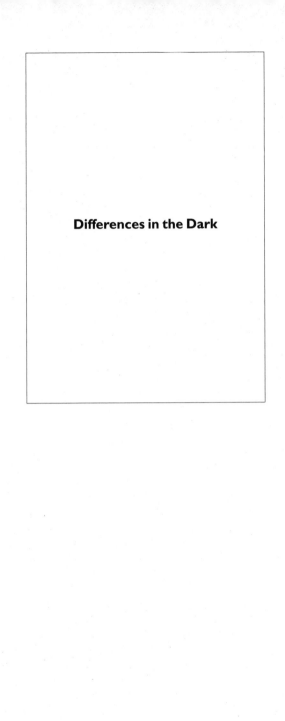

# Differences in the Dark

## Differences in the Dark
### American Movies and English Theater

The theater and the movies are many things: livelihoods, styles of entertainment, social occasions, lucrative industries. They are also cultural lexicons, art forms on which are inscribed the histories and inclinations of particular peoples. The most obvious instance of this mating of nationality with aesthetics might be the movie western. A subgenre devised by Americans at the cinema's dawn, the story of settling the wilderness had literary antecedents in this country stretching back to James Fenimore Cooper and his *Leatherstocking Tales*. With its focus on the clash between civilization and savagery, the familiar and the unknown, and with its interest in codes of masculinity, the early movie western met the needs of a society just a generation removed from continental expansion. The form has outlived memories of the frontier. Hollywood filmmakers continue to spruce up their balance sheets with the profits from space-age permutations, sagas of extraterrestrial travel and warfare with aliens.

But subject matter or content is not the only, and perhaps not the most important, index of national preference. An artistic medium may enjoy a special bond with a given social order through its modes of production and consumption. The cinema is a twentieth-century phenomenon that relies on technology, demands huge expenditures of capital, and overrides spatial and temporal boundaries. Movies appeal to a mass public and are absorbed in the darkness and silence of multiplex screening rooms. Intermissions, once the rule for double features, no longer vary the experience. Movies discourage personal connection, either among spectators and actors or among members of the audience. If watched at home, with a VCR, the immaterial images undergo a physical hardening or metamorphosis into the tangible commodity form of the videocassette.

The theater, by way of contrast, is an ancient institution that may avail itself of modern technologies but hardly requires them. Its one essential component is the human player. Dramas can be read as books, possessed as objects, but each act of theatergoing is a unique and personalized event that cannot be mechanically duplicated. To attend a stage play is, ideally, to be part of a group. The public has paid its money to see real men and women, not images, and the feeling of contact on both sides can be intense: just as the spectators are stirred by the performers (which happens at the movies too), so the performers respond to the mood and quality of attention from the audience. The ceremony of intermission ties the viewers to each other. But all this oneness comes at a price, and in dollar terms it is a higher price than most people can afford. The movies are popular entertainment, while the theater is normally elite.

What I have sketched here, using fairly conventional categories, are not just two artistic modalities but the profiles of two societies, the United States and Great Britain. While generalizations about nations are notoriously risky, one might venture the following: Americans are the global front-runners in technology. In economic might they have competitors but no equal. They are the standard-bearers of cultural modernity, in all the negative as well as positive resonances of that word: materialism, privatism, rootlessness, anomie, and individualism have taken hold in this country with a virulence that strikes many observers as unprecedented. But America is also among the world's leaders in opportunities for its citizens. Ideologically (if not always in practice), it is the homeland of democratic principles, a society without ascriptive rank that naturalized the dogma of egalitarianism.

The British nation preserves royalty on the threshold of the twenty-first century, and its parliament allots seats to hereditary lords. These atavisms refute the idea of inherent human equality. Yet at the same time, many Britons have a sense of national cohesion that has been nurtured by their geographical insularity and by the long-standing (though now changing) racial uniformity of their population. Witness the quite extraordinary festivities to commemorate the fiftieth anniversary of Britain's victory in World War II, a celebration of communal spirit tinged with nostalgia for vanished greatness. And the British, though once the wedge of the Industrial Revolution, no longer signify the modern. Guidebooks describe them as a literate people who cherish tradition and concreteness. Their greatest philosophic and scientific minds—Locke, Newton, Darwin—have been empiricists who prized reality.

The motion pictures and the theater, in short, are but two of multiple loci where the different emphases of American and English culture make themselves manifest. The screen encapsulates a leaning to disembodied modernity, while the stage expresses a commitment to embodiment and a respect for shared heritage. Of course this overly schematic dichotomy admits of exceptions. Neither art forms nor cultures are unitary. "National character," as that concept is used here, does not denote anything inborn; it refers, rather, to the complex of belief and behavior that has been constructed by a people's historical experience and by social, economic, and political forces. Such contructions are shot through with ideology. They alter over time. The English, to mention an obvious example, have not always been so attached to the drama as they are at present. In the seventeenth century, English sectarians closed London's stages as lewd and ungodly spectacles. But with the monarchy's backing, the playhouses reopened during the Restoration, and the antitheatrical prejudice, brought with them by Puritan exiles, waxed in the New World long after it had ebbed in the Old.[1]

The two media, theater and film, are especially revealing sites of difference. This is so because the variations in national outlook explored in this essay came to a head at a particular juncture in history, the period during which the movies were developed. Cinema and drama embarked on their dissimilar trajectories just when the United States began to eclipse Great Britain as an industrial and international power. Not that the two arts have ever been interchangeable. This study most definitely does not revive the obsolete understanding of early film as an outgrowth of the Victorian stage's quest for pictorial realism.[2] The movies absorbed a plurality of influences, the stage being just one among them, but it is nevertheless the case that the cinema's drift toward diegetic storytelling inverted the movement of the drama away from hermetic self-enclosure. The two forms have followed contrary paths in the twentieth century, not because they reacted against each other's supposed capabilites, but rather because they evolved in unison with the destinies of the nation-states with which they were most closely identified.

But is it not anachronistic, in this era of borderless capitalism, to speculate about the "nationality" of either theater or film? The Chicago-born playwright Richard Nelson resides in London and has his work performed by the Royal Shakespeare Company; musicals by the Englishman Andrew Lloyd Webber appear regularly on Broadway. Portability or the occluding of provenance is even more extreme with the cinema. Movies with American financing have been shot at locations all over the globe and feature French, Italian, English, Russian, and Indian actors. Warner Brothers put up the money for *Batman* but arranged to have the picture shot at London's Pinewood Studios in order to take advantage of the favorable exchange rates prevailing at the time (1988). The screenwriter, producer, and many of the actors came over from the United States, but the British supplied the crew and technical staff, including the designers who built the set for Gotham City. The prevalence of such joint ventures has prompted the English film director David Puttnam to dismiss talk of national attribution as "hopelessly out-of-date now."[3]

Puttnam badly overstates the matter. Decentralized, global filmmaking has not eliminated American control but merely reconfigured it. Hollywood continues to provide the cash and dominates the mechanisms of distribution and marketing. Americans have a preponderant say in what scripts make it to the screen, who stars in the pictures, and how much is spent to promote them. "Post-Fordist" production, as it has been called, turns out to coexist quite happily with unprecedented concentration. It has left largely undisturbed the colonizing of world cinema by the United States.

As for the theater, Richard Nelson's partiality for London should surprise no one. That city's hospitality to the drama is legendary: what better place for a serious playwright to practice his calling? Webber's international success testifies to the musical's return to the setting of its former glory. In the nineteenth century, the team of W. S. Gilbert and Arthur Sullivan had a prolific career as authors of satiric musical comedies, Anglicized versions of the French opéra bouffe. One could mention too, as an indication of London's theatrical genius, the bumper crop of Tony Awards garnered in 1997 by the British revival of Ibsen's *A Doll's House* (Janet McTeer as best actress, Owen Teale as best featured actor, and Anthony Page as best director).

To dwell on the breach between two peoples who, in George Bernard Shaw's famous quip, are separated by a common language, is inevitably to scant the similarities or, better yet, the continuities that knit them together. One could build a case for seeing the United States as a kind of fulfillment of certain tendencies in British culture. Take Britain's tardiness in assimilating the Second Industrial Revolution. The delay gave America an enormous head start in cinematic innovation. But a century earlier the English had been the first out of the gate, the preeminent modernizing society in the West. Having initiated the Industrial Revolution, the English bequeathed to their New World cousins the technological know-how that in the long run enabled Americans to outstrip them economically. Margaret Thatcher's enthusiasm about the "special relationship" between the United Kingdom and the United States, which for her mandated a repudiation of Europe, contained an important truth. The long symbiosis between the erstwhile global epicenter and its transatlantic offshoot performed the vital historical service of midwifing America's emergence as the dominant industrial and imperial force of the late twentieth century.

It would be possible to argue, then, that the galaxy of attitudes associated in this essay with American society and the cinema is not so much a deviation from the Anglo-theatrical prototype as a legacy. Rejection of community, technological utopianism, and the imperialism of free trade—these are elaborations of proclivities inherited from the British. Self-reliance, after all, was a virtue of John Bull's before Americans from Emerson to the present domesticated it as a test of patriotism. (British followers of Thatcher, blaming welfarism for their country's economic woes, have tried to repatriate the habit, and "New Labour's" Tony Blair has blessed the project.) Birmingham ironworks hatched Pittsburgh steel mills. And apart from ancient Rome, fin-de-siècle expansionists looked to Great Britain for their model of empire. The sun never set on the Union Jack well before the American colonies were strong enough to covet territory beyond their borders.

Nor should it be forgotten that the English themselves are avid consumers of the movies. (So, too, throngs of American tourists patronize the Strand, eager to sample the plays they are missing at home.) However much Britons may cherish their theatrical past, when they go in search of entertainment, most make the same choices that Americans do. As a people they spend far more annually on the cinema than the drama, and the pictures they queue up to see are made by Hollywood. In 1995, not one of the top ten grossing films in the United Kingdom was domestically produced; leading the list were *Batman Forever*, *Casper*, and *Braveheart*.

Grant the legacies. Grant, too, that the lure of American popular culture transcends nationality. I would still insist that the divisions between England and America, as between the drama and the movies, are as salient as the linkages. The English may have flocked to watch Val Kilmer and Jim Carrey, but elsewhere in their daily lives, their politics, and their pastimes they continue to opt for choices that dilute their philo-Americanism. They even impart a distinctively British spin to cinematic culture: they manufacture films and attend them in ways that suggest the influence of the theater.

One could say that the stage is a nodal point of resistance to English society's own "Americanizing" urges. (Bracket, for the time being, the experimental theater.) The legitimate stage upholds customary values against the possible future symbolized by the movies. It connotes the obstinate retention of orality, eloquence, and community. It is a beseiged but still formidable pillar of firmness against the rush to turn the British Isles into a facsimile and willing satellite of the United States. One cannot dispose of the drama's significance for the English by simply waving it aside as an exclusive residue in an otherwise demotic or mass culture. Exclusive it definitely is, but that hierarchical dimension is one measure of its representativeness. Whether in London or New York, relatively well-to-do people buy theater tickets. But among the English, it is not just playgoers who share the theater's values.

When I speak in this essay of "the theater" or "the movies," it should be clear that I am referring to mainstream or commercial institutions. What concerns me is how the dominant cultural typologies register and influence nationality. No attention is paid to alternative or fringe formats and how these might problematize the heuristic opposition of stage and screen. So readers will look in vain—to mention only the movies—for material on low-budget films, or pornography, or documentaries, or the Yiddish cinema, or avant-garde and non-narrative film, or race moviemakers like Oscar Micheaux, or the blaxploitation pictures, most released in the early seventies, that starred Richard Roundtree. To do full justice to these peripheral developments would require a separate study.

But while I focus on the main currents, I do not mean to suggest that the stage and the cinema *had* to take the primary forms that they did. The styles we think of as classical Hollywood or the West End were not preordained, not dictated by the unfolding of a technological imperative or by the supineness of the medium before a given social system. They were the result of chance, circumstance, and human decisions; and other decisions could have been made. The theater and the movies may have sympathies one way or the other, but nothing in their natures or their favored nationalities requires them to be either participatory or passive and anonymous. As I show in some detail, the two arts have changed throughout history, shuttling across a range of possible identities, and their unpredictability belies any notion of determinism.

Besides omitting discussion of maverick cinema and drama, I give little notice to television. The small box gets mentioned only in passing as a threat to moviegoing in the 1950s and as a catalyst to the widescreen revolution. I do not explore the rather obvious divergences between American and English television—schisms that have narrowed in the last few decades with the introduction of commercial broadcasting to Britain and the importing of the highest rated American shows. Owing to the long dominance of the BBC and its fairly highbrow roster of programs, English television until recently maintained something of the character of the stage—in addition to the usual sit-coms, a certain fastidious superiority to unbridled capitalism and an investment in uplifting popular taste through the adaptation of "masterpieces." English TV was—and, in a measure, still is—to the thoroughly commodified American brand of TV as the London theater is to the movies.4

More than this, critics of American television have charged the cathode tube with eroding the sociability of moviegoing by sequestering people in their homes. According to this view, the once mighty cinema is itself a kind of theatrical, obsolescent medium, and television the movielike, modernizing scourge supplanting common experience with privatism and isolation. Another view holds that television's own history replays a drama-to-motion pictures succession. In the so-called Network Era (roughly 1955 to 1985), 90 percent of the viewing audience tuned in to the same three channels, CBS, NBC, and ABC. Broadcasting brought people together, runs the argument, and created a common culture: it "was a national theater for a nation that emphatically refused to have one." Then the VCR and cable appeared on the scene, and the unity of televisual culture splintered apart. Television as American mass theater gave way to TV as the atomized cinema.5

Still other claims about television's relevance to the topics discussed in this essay could be proposed. But for the most part I do not address them. There are several reasons for my reticence. First, although I comment on some of the ways American theater approximates the (American) movies, and English cinema the (West End) drama, I am not primarily interested in national intonations within the same medium. My concern, rather, is to show how the two forms of entertainment, stage and screen, became affiliated with *different* nationalities. To include television would be to change the focus. For as a cultural environment, television cannot be conflated with either the theater or motion pictures, even the pictures that are televised or shown through the VCR. As Raymond Williams pointed out more than twenty years ago, television is a structure, not of discrete units, but of "flow," of programs following one another in sequence. It is a third media operation characterized by fluidity, as opposed to the theater's evanescence and film's autonomy, and adequate treatment of its distinctive attributes would, once again, require a separate study.6

Several friends who read this book in manuscript remarked on my indebtedness to Walter Benjamin, especially his great essay on the evacuation of aura in the epoch of mechanized art, and to Jacques Derrida, who has so forcefully championed writing's "absence" against the supposedly pure immediacy of speech. I am happy to acknowledge the influence of these two theorists. My methodology, however, is eclectic and latitudinarian, and I would argue that my emphasis on the cinema's nonreciprocity owes less to any particular thinker than to the obvious character of the medium. I would further suggest—in an attempt to "Benjaminize" Derrida, that is, to historicize his insights—that the Frenchman's devaluation of orality and presence are themselves a corol-

lary of late twentieth-century technological developments. Derrida rein-
scribes as a positive philosophical value the disembodiment begun with
motion pictures and accelerating, in the decades when he first came to
notice, with the popularizing of the VCR and the invasion of the home
by computers.7 It seems relevant that these changes first swept the
United States before catching on elsewhere. Derrida's prestige in the
land of Hollywood and Microsoft exceeds his stature in his native
France. His disrepute in England, though moderated of late, is still substantial, and altogether of a piece with British loyalty to the theater and
suspicion of immateriality.

Something should be said about the style and structure of the book. Both
are unconventional. I modulate between a conversational mode and a
more theoretical voice, interspersing personal experiences and historical data. The reminiscences cluster at the outset because the London
interlude they describe was germinative of the entire project. And while
the organization is more random and paratactic than usual scholarly
texts, the sections, some quite short, others of essay length, ultimately
cohere into a larger argument.

   It will be noticed that I slip into the habit of using "English" and
"British" without distinction. I plead guilty to laxness on this score,
but cite in my defense the alternation of the terms in ordinary speech,
"which," as Perry Anderson has said, "it remains pedantic to scout
altogether."8 Still, the English stage is a fairly centralized institution,
with its riches concentrated in London and Stratford, and I apologize
if anything I have written misrepresents the Scots, Welsh, or Northern
Irish.

   Finally, I want to anticipate a possible objection that I have not been
forthright enough in teasing out the political implications of the
America-movies/England-drama contrast. Another way of putting this
would be that my own position on the contrast remains ambiguous. It
might appear to some readers that I have oversold the virtues of English
communitarianism. Other readers might detect a chauvinistic bias
toward the cinematic ethos and its American breeding ground. My
intention, as an American (and an Americanist) who loves Britain, has
been to render the pluses and drawbacks on both sides. But the issues

are too important, and too intertwined with my thesis, to leave their summing up to the reader's inference. I have therefore appended a brief afterword in an effort to clarify the politics of Anglo-American cultural divergence—and my ambivalence about them.

## Dreams and Memories

Are dreams cinematic or theatrical? Which is memory? When I close my eyes, and summon up an image from last week, a couple of friends walking beside me on a crowded street, is the experience similar to sitting in a blackened auditorium before an enclosed rectangle, in luminous color, with vivid, hyperrealistic details, and the roar of traffic on the sound track? Moving pictures are often said to work like dreams or memory, with flattened simulations, fade-outs and close-ups, time compressed or expanded, the restrictions of space overcome. It is no coincidence that the 1890s, the decade when the movies were invented in France and the United States, witnessed the birth of psychoanalysis as a therapeutic technique, an exploration into the boundless recesses of internal space to complement the cinema's conquest of external nature. Or is the remembered image I behold in my mind more like a scene from a play, with none of the clarity and exactness produced by technology? I can make out two rather hazy figures flanking a third form, a lack of clear-cut borders, and silence save for the sound of voices conversing. When I watch a movie, my vision and hearing are flawless; but sitting in a theater, say in Row RR Center, I am aware of the limitations of my perception, or more precisely my body, my less-than-perfect eyesight, my difficulty in hearing hushed tones at a distance of more than a dozen feet. I open my eyes, and the picture vanishes: is it a screen that has gone dark, or a curtain that has descended?

## Recollections of a London Theatergoer

I enjoy the theater and try to attend plays in the United States, though I don't get to as many as I would like. An occasional trip to New York City to see a Broadway show, maybe three or four visits annually to the American Repertory Theater in Cambridge, to catch *The Tempest* or *Six Characters in Search of an Author*. If I have a craving to see Shakespeare, I am just as likely to go to the local multiplex, now that Kenneth Branagh has started making movies of such high quality. But in London, on a recent sabbatical, I became an enthusiast of the stage, attending at least a play a week, dragging my wife and daughters to obscure performances of obscure dramas, refusing to see an American movie at all, although I did take in several English films, including a murder mystery called *Shallow Grave* (1994).

The change wasn't in me but in the environment. No tourist can fail to notice it: in contrast to American cities like Boston or New York, where cultural life, even that of intellectuals, is saturated with the movies, in London the premier art form is the theater. (I am excluding, for the moment, television and the VCR.) It may be going too far to say that theater dominates English middle- and highbrow culture, but with playhouse prices considerably lower than in the United States, and movie tickets a good bit higher—six or seven pounds in 1995, or as much as ten dollars for a first-run feature, when American cinemas were charging six or seven dollars—the stage can more than hold its own against the silver screen. Among other things favoring it, there is the justifiable pride among the English at still being, in the words of Diana Rigg, "the capital of the theatre world."9 Few Londoners would say the same about English literature, its glory now largely departed to former colonies and other races. And despite the satisfaction in claiming Emma Thompson, James Ivory (who is actually American), and Alfred Hitchcock (expatriated to the United States), even fewer would dispute the cinematic preeminence of Hollywood. No less a cultural arbiter than the magazine *Vanity Fair* has reached the same conclusion: against American monopoly of the film industry, asserts a recent article, using a formulation I will return to, Britain is the "Empire of the Stage."10

It certainly seemed that way to me on my weekly forays to the South Bank or the Royal Court. I saw Tom Stoppard's *Arcadia* and *Indian Ink*, David Hare's *Skylight*, the Theatre de Complicite's *The Three Lives of Lucie Cabrol*, Sam Shepard's *Sympatico*. (The English stage Shepard and

Arthur Miller as often, or more often, than do their countrymen. They even stage Wallace Shawn, whose works can't find a venue in the United States.) I saw revivals of *The Three Penny Opera, Love's Labour's Lost, A Midsummer Night's Dream, Hamlet,* and Sean O'Casey's *The Silver Tassie.* I attended such an abundance of plays that many of the details now escape me, but two experiences from that time stand out, perhaps because they seem to exemplify the difference between the theater as an English cultural idiom and the cinema as the embodiment of something intensely American.

The first experience is the one I remember most fully: it took place at the King's Head, a pub on Upper Street, located between a Ryman's stationery store and the Islington post office. I happened upon this alternative theater space, whose existence dates back to 1971, quite by accident. I was on my way to the post office to buy airmail stamps when a protest demonstration brought me to a halt in front of the pub door. The Conservatives had announced plans to consolidate metropolitan postal facilities, and picketers had assembled outside the Islington branch, leafleting passersby and demanding the retention of neighborhood services.

With denunciations of John Major's government ringing in my ears, I noticed placards advertising *The Secret Garden,* to be performed at the King's Head as a musical beginning the next week. I had seen the American film made by Agnieszka Holland from the Frances Hodgson Burnett novel about a year before, and my two daughters had enjoyed it so much that we had bought the video. It would be fun, I thought, to take them to the Saturday matinee; the price, a bargain by American standards, was six pounds a ticket, and what could be a more authentically English setting for the drama than a shabby pub in North London?

I have preserved the mimeographed eight-page playbill from that production, so I know that the book and lyrics were by Diana Morgan, the music by Steven Markwick, and the part of Mary Lennox played by a young actress named Katey Crawford Kastin. These people were not amateurs: most had appeared on radio and television as well as in other London theaters; several had movie credits; and the director, an American, had produced more than two hundred works at the King's

Head. The musical was presented in a windowless room at the rear of the pub, with a makeshift stage in front, a group of tables with chairs, and a row of seats in the back. The room wasn't large—it could accommodate about eighty, I would guess—and it didn't resemble any theater I had been in before. It had the look and feel of an abandoned warehouse, and it was cold enough to keep your coat on. At the end of the performance, the director came out on stage and delivered an impassioned plea for contributions to the King's Head building fund.

The play, which didn't try to emulate the movie's realism, charmed my daughters, and the acting, as always in London, was remarkably polished, but what has stayed with me most from that afternoon are two quite extraneous matters: the sense of intimacy in that uninviting space, and the appearance of the slim teenager who was cast as Mary Lennox. The lights were lowered but remained on. People drank lager, whispered, and exchanged looks. Dilapidated chairs creaked. No proscenium arch demarcated the stage, and the actors made no pretense of ignoring the "fourth wall," as the watching audience came to be known in the nineteenth century. The actress playing Mrs. Medlock repeatedly smiled at the children seated in front of her. All this was distracting enough, in a pleasant way; even more so was the small birthmark, a dime-sized patch of brown hair, under the right eye of Katey Kastin. This disfiguring touch of nature, as conspicuous as the pinkish scrawl atop Gorbachev's head, or the tiny crimson hand in Nathaniel Hawthorne's famous story, "The Birthmark," fascinated and somewhat disconcerted my daughters, who wondered what it was and felt slightly self-conscious for its unembarrassed owner. An aspiring American actress, especially one with Kastin's singing ability, would almost certainly have had the discoloration surgically removed.[11]

A palpable feeling of community, linking performers and audience, and a deference to the decrees of nature, in the artistic medium that still relies on human material, the presence of the actor and actress: these were recurrent motifs in my six months' adventure as a theatergoer. The holding on to nature, a national proclivity that would, at first glance, seem more true of Americans, proved upon reflection to be highly characteristic of the English. Not only do they treasure live performance, they make a cult of their public and family gardens, play their version of football on natural, never artificial, surface, and retain grass at their national tennis championship at Wimbledon, allowing the green sward to impart unpredictable bounces to serve and volley.

The affirmation of community is hardly confined to unorthodox locations like the King's Head. An ethos of interaction pervades London theater—more muted in the West End, where intermission still gives audience members an opportunity to mingle, to chat, and to be seen, and very marked in subsidized playhouses such as the National and the Barbican, where actors routinely clap for the audience while being applauded themselves. The desire to establish intimacy is so integral to the stage that it can become contrived, scripted into the production rather than permitted to emerge spontaneously. This was the case with my second memory, once again of a Saturday matinee I attended with my daughters, a revival by the Royal Shakespeare Company of Carlo Goldoni's eighteenth-century comedy, *The Venetian Twins*.

The price per ticket was higher this time, thirteen pounds or about twenty dollars, and the seating was stratified, as it usually is at the theater; you got the view you paid for. But every effort was made to join hands across that class-divided audience: there were frequent jokey exchanges between the performers and the public, some of whom had been invited to sit at tables on the stage. (At least I think they were members of the public; it's possible they were extras.) On one occasion, a character flubbed a line, apparently by accident, and a second character exclaimed, "Don't worry. It's only a matinee." A man in the audience coughed and cleared his throat, and an actor remarked, "I didn't know we let in sea lions." And during a sword fight, the combatants ran into the front seats and ran through a spectator in the first row, who was carried to the stage amid calls for a doctor and great expressions of concern.

If this horseplay was a little too much, it also formed a stark contrast to the experience of watching a movie, and the disparity, I came to realize, was part, parhaps a large part, of the point. The London theater, whatever else it might be, is not American; it strives to maintain its cultural identity against the perceived imperialism of Hollywood. The English cinema, always overshadowed by its more robust overseas competitor, displays something of the same independence, or perhaps jingoism, to use a term that was first coined in the music halls of Queen

Victoria's time.[12] As many students of the medium have observed, English movies tend to reproduce the trademarks of the English stage, from a preference for filming adaptations of well-known literary works to an emphasis on classical acting.

*Shallow Grave*, the mystery I saw at the Screen on Baker Street, bears out the generic congruence. This movie seems at first to have all the earmarks of a violent Hollywood thriller. Three Yuppie roommates in Glasgow steal the money of a dead gangster, have to kill the gangster's accomplices to protect themselves, and then start eliminating each other. One of them saws off the hands and feet of the corpses to prevent identification. He uses a hammer to crush in the skulls of the dead men. The character named Alex (played by Ewan McGregor, since familiar to Americans for his role in *Trainspotting*, 1996) is pinioned to the floor when another character (the woman Juliet) pounds a knife blade through his shoulder with her shoe. Bright red blood splatters on enamel and wood.

Gore aside, *Shallow Grave* is a low-budget, tightly crafted film that could have been a play. The filmmakers respect the unities of time and space, about three-quarters of the action occurring indoors, in the apartment shared by the young friends. Shots of pastel walls, winding stairwells, white-sheeted beds, bathrooms, and doors fill up the screen. Nobody is inarticulate. The three main characters exchange witty repartee. All belong to the well-educated classes: a chartered accountant, a newspaper reporter, a medical intern. The accountant retreats from the apartment to an attic loft, into the floor of which he drills holes to spy on his friends. An atmosphere of claustrophobia and entrapment pervades the movie, as if on some level it were about its own confinements.

English movie houses, like English movies, take their lead from the theater. At Baker Street, patrons are assigned a seat number when they purchase a ticket, sparing them the scramble for seating familiar to American cinemas. At other London movie houses, like the Curzon Mayfair, ticket prices are staggered on the theatrical model. Americans charge staggered prices at sporting events and concerts, but no popular entertainment is so American as the movies, and there the nation's cultural space is egalitarian, or pretends to be, with a single price charged for all. A strict separation is preserved between the spectators and the action

depicted on the screen. English cultural space is hierarchical *and* participatory, with seating determined by wealth but an appreciation of common
purpose uniting viewer and performer. Is this the difference, in short-
hand, between the United States, a democracy and global power, and
Great Britain, a constitutional monarchy on the long slope of its decline?

## Random Parallels Between the Cinema and America

One of the earliest treatises about the movies is a little volume published in 1915 by the American poet Vachel Lindsay, *The Art of the Moving
Picture*. This eccentric book, a trove of information and spirited argument, takes up several of the themes I will be pursuing here. For example, Lindsay remarks on the similarity in elite reaction to the movies and
the novel, both art forms having aroused the wrath of critics as a threat
to morality. Is the cinema the incitement to illicit behavior its pious
detractors charge it with being? Not so, Lindsay says: films, in his view,
actually contribute to temperance by siphoning immigrant and working-class customers away from the saloons. More than this, the movies
are a positive force for spiritual transformation, a "new weapon of men"
that has the power to change "the face of the whole earth." Lindsay's
book pulsates with the millennial fantasies the movies inspired in their
infancy and inspire to this day: visions of Hollywood, as the omphalos
of the "photoplay," guiding humanity into a future of "immemorial wonder."[13] (This apocalyptic nationalism, a translation of centuries-old
American messianic dreams into the register of mass culture, will
require further comment later on.)

An entire chapter of *The Art of the Moving Picture* is devoted to list-
ing "Thirty Differences between the Photoplays and the Stage." I have
read these pages several times, and always with perplexing results; as
the differences are not numbered, I have yet to discover the advertised
total. Some are fairly obvious, such as reliance on visual images instead
of words. (The book appeared in the era of silent pictures.) Others are
more unexpected, as when, after identifying films with "speed-mania,"
Lindsay announces that no movie should last more than an hour, in con-

trast to the two and a half hours of the typical drama.[14]

Inspired by Lindsay's example, I have compiled my own list about the movies. Mine consists of similarities between the silver screen and the United States, and I will use selected examples from classic American literature, as well as classics written about America by foreigners, for evidence of national traits. I have not numbered the list, and depending on how and what one counts, there are either fewer or more than thirty items. But Lindsay appears to have cheated on that score himself.

## Speed/Modernity

"Speed-mania": the mechanically produced power, not merely to capture motion on celluloid but, by cutting and splicing, to jump from one physical location to another in an instant. What term better describes the current century? Reflections on the modern invariably single out the increased pace of activity, the quickened character of life under conditions of constant change. And no nation has been more closely associated with ceaseless movement and technological daring than the United States.

American culture abounds in harrowing visions of speed, of rushing bodies and jolting collisions. The profusion of nonstop images antedates the cinema. In Edgar Allen Poe's 1840 tale, "The Man of the Crowd," the jostles of the metropolitan mass become emblematic of the shocks of daily life, the experience, say, of a working man on a fast-moving assembly line. Poe's horror and mystery stories, such as those featuring his Parisian detective, C. Auguste Dupin, subject the reader to a similar kind of battering, with one unforeseen or frightening development following another in rapid succession.[15]

As Poe wrote, the first railroads began to connect the Atlantic seaboard. Before the century was over, the great transcontinental lines gave the United States the world lead in rail mileage. Among the many ties between the mechanized colossus and the movies, one might mention the visual experience of hurtling through the landscape in an iron carriage. Sounds and smells disappeared as the scenery shot by, just as they did in the first motion pictures, and concrete things lost their tactility. The spectator-traveler observed the passing sights through the frame of the compartment window, as though he or she were watching images projected on a bordered rectangle. To heighten the parallel, objects in the foreground blurred, as they do when one sits in close proximity to the screen, while those in the background acquired a panoramic evanescence. The earliest motion pictures tapped into this association with rail travel. Some theaters were designed as train cars, with conductors taking tickets and the sound effects of wheels and hissing steam. More dramatically, the spectator was repositioned on the track rather than within the flying projectile. Patrons seated in the darkened room were startled to see the smoke-spewing engines barreling down upon them.[16]

Walter Benjamin, who memorably analyzed Poe's modernism, regarded Paris as the capital of the nineteenth century. If America's most dynamic city, New York, with its futuristic skyline and vastly speeded-up rhythms, is the capital of the twentieth century, will Los Angeles, the metropolis of the moving image, be the capital of the twenty-first?[17] Certainly the movies, with their technique of accelerated montage (perfected in the music videos of today), have replaced fictions like Poe's as the medium best adapted to the hectic tempo of modernity.

But whether next century's movies are actually made in Hollywood is irrelevant. The flexibility of post-Fordist cinema reaffirms the genre's spatial and temporal unboundedness. The mode of production, in other words, has finally caught up with the revolutionary dislocations of space and time registered by the camera. This development in the global political economy can paradoxically be regarded as consistent with the cinema's Americanism. For the United States has shown the way in upending conventional experience of temporal order and distance.

## Time and Space

America has always claimed to represent escape from history. The country has defined itself, against the ancient lands of Europe, as a new beginning and equated its promise with the availability of "free soil," the vast expanse of unsettled territory to the west. The movies likewise privilege space and treat temporal sequence with cavalier disdain. Film not only brings limitless space into the circumscribed auditorium, exhibiting images of outdoor scenes that could not appear on the stage— mountains, oceans, the wilderness—it also uses distance and direction to create meaning, as in the close-up, the long shot, upward movement of the camera to suggest aspiration or happiness, circular movement to convey dizziness, and so on. Space doesn't have the same significance in theater because the viewer's position remains fixed with regard to the stage.

So, too, film disintegrates or reshuffles time more readily than theater, through the use of flashback, flash forward, slow motion, montage, and cutting. The duration of the literal event, and the time required to watch it, are usually the same in drama; but cinematic time is often discontinuous with the action portrayed, as when a three-course meal is consumed in a scene lasting a minute, or a coast-to-coast airplane flight requires only a few seconds.

Superiority or indifference to chronological coherence applies to the movie actor as well. In theater, events unfold in sequence, and the actor or actress must memorize an entire performance. Screen performers have little need to call on memory: they are responsible only for the lines for the day's shooting, and scenes are often shot out of order, without regard for the narrative continuity that will be supplied by an editor in the cutting room.[18]

Freedom in space, emancipation from linear time and history: the movies provide a version of experience akin to that found in landmarks of American identity like J. Hector St. John de Crèvecoeur's *Letters from an American Farmer* (1782) and the poetry of Walt Whitman. Crèvecoeur's book, published a year before the Treaty of Paris and the formal recognition of American independence (and long before the moving pictures were dreamt of), can be taken as foundational of the national disposition to displace the temporal with the spatial. The American, asserts Crèvecoeur, is a "new man" who sloughs off Europe and the past by trekking westward to possess himself of fertile land. The expanse of virgin wilderness, being ostensibly infinite, ensures that civilization, with its accumulated ills, can never catch up with the always mobile pioneer.

## Size (and Space Again)

The cinema has flourished in the United States because of the country's demographic and geographic enormity. *Demography* first: America's population, after the breakup of the Soviet Union, is the largest of the advanced industrial nations, and exceeded only by China's and India's among underdeveloped societies. At two hundred and sixty-three million (as of 1995), it is four and a half times as great as Britain's population (fifty-eight million) and almost the equal of Western Europe's. Moreover, the pace of divergence between America and Britain has quickened since the cinema's invention. In 1890, England, Scotland, and Wales had a combined population of about 33 million; the United States doubled that with 63 million. By 1924, the figures were 43 and 114 million; and by 1950, when America's overtaking of Britain as global colossus was apparent to all, the ratio was three to one (150 to 49 million). For the movies, these numbers have added up to prosperity: Hollywood had a ready-made domestic market big enough to justify high expenditures and to generate even higher profits. The great returns attracted investment, which funded expansion and modernizing advances like sound and color, which in turn attracted new moviegoers from the ever-growing populace. America's physical amplitude absorbed these demographic increases without difficulty.

*Geography.* An observation by Vachel Lindsay suggests another relationship between large terrain and the cinema: "The big social fact about the moving picture is that it is scattered like the newspaper."[19] Film can be distributed anywhere; its stars and glamour not only travel but can appear in many places at the same time. This ubiquity gives it an incalculable advantage over the drama in a republic the size of a continent, where distances are too great to pay regular vists to a cultural capital like London in order to see "original" productions. There *are* no original productions in the movies.[20]

It would seem to follow, then, that space can be as determinative as time or history in sponsoring mechanical progress. That is, new technologies arise, not merely because scientific knowledge, building upon the achievements of the past, has reached a certain state of ripeness, but because impediments of magnitude mandate breakthroughs that would otherwise remain unnecessary. Benjamin, in his influential essay on "The Work of Art in the Age of Mechanical Reproduction," announces in his very title his prejudice toward the temporal as the crucial motivation for superseding presence. An American view of the subject, however, might emphasize the spatial incentive for the adoption of art forms that rely on repeatability.[21]

This way of thinking, which ascribes creative power to size or space, is in fact a hoary American mental habit. It stretches back at least to Crèvecoeur, but its most renowned exponent is Frederick Jackson Turner, the historian who elevated the idea of spatial causality into a theory of national development. Turner's thesis held that space in the guise of vacant territory dictated the nature of American freedom's unfolding over time. As it happens, he arrived at this insight just as the movies burst upon the national scene, in the 1890s, a decade he referred to as the most momentous in our history. The new species of popular entertainment amounted to a parallel demonstration of Turner's theory: its extension in space beyond anything dreamed of in the theater revolutionized its deployment of temporal sequence.

In an essay called "Contributions of the West to American Democracy," Turner zeroed in on four profound changes occurring in the 1890s. (Substitute "cinema" for "democracy," and we have our variation on Benjamin's title.) The first was the closing of the frontier. In second place, Turner listed the "concentration of capital" giving rise to industrial combination. His third change was overseas expansion, the momentum for which, Turner surmised, sprang from the drying up of available western land. And the final phenomenon was the spread of socialism or Populism, a political movement inextricable from the previous three occurrences.[22]

Every one of these developments, which for Turner were reshaping American identity, has a significant relation to the cinema. The frontier's vanishing, and the accompanying growth of imperialism, will be examined later. The forms taken by American capitalism, impelled in its course by "the problem of magnitude" (in Turner's words),[23] and the failed political protest against that direction, will detain us here. Scale too gigantic for personal control will be shown to be as symptomatic of American business as "derealized" presence is of the movies.

## Styles of Capitalism

The 1890s were the turning point of industrial capitalism. The competitive, proprietary type of enterprise, for over a century the engine of national growth, yielded in a relatively few years to the corporate, administrative system that has powered the American economy ever since. Populism, the party of agriculture and the small enterprise, went down to defeat before the forces favoring giant companies in which management was split off from ownership. This restructuring was the equivalent in business affairs of the supercession in the cultural realm of the stage by the movies; more, its American outcome inverted the English pattern, where an allegiance to personal capitalism and gentry values successfully resisted the trend toward impersonality.

The decade was inaugurated by the Sherman Antitrust Act of 1890. Some historians have interpreted this act as encouraging a result contrary to its stated purpose: the law prohibited European-style cartels and thus abetted economic mergers. But the role of statute in inflecting American capitalism took a back seat to geographical pressure. Not only did the United States have the largest and fastest-growing domestic market in the world, its population was scattered across immensities of space. The same physical circumstances supporting film over theater gave industrial organization an expansive cast. Meeting the requirements of "scale and scope" necessitated complex, dynamic businesses with armies of managers and huge capital outlays.

The rush to consolidation, antedating the Panic of 1893, got under way in earnest with recovery in 1897. By 1904 one third of all companies in the country had been absorbed into larger units. The United States Steel Corporation, organized in 1901, was one of the largest, with eleven constituent producers and stock valued at $1.5 billion. (The prototypes for this kind of far-flung, heavily capitalized enterprise were the railroad and telegraph networks, vaster than anything in Europe, that had knitted the continent together after the Civil War.) Designated "managerial capitalism" by the business historian Alfred D. Chandler, the American style of corporation was so massive and diversified that it rendered direct ownership obsolete. Hands-on operation by owner-entrepreneurs, the nineteenth-century rule, was supplanted by impersonal administration by salaried executives.[24]

British firms stuck more closely to the older—one might say, more intimate—institutional system. A decisive factor here was the smallness and compactness of the island kingdom. As early as 1851, one half of Britain's population was clustered in towns of five thousand or more, a ratio not equaled in the United States until 1960. English corporations did not have to emulate the size and complexity of their American counterparts in order to service so concentrated a consumer market. Giant mail-order retailers like Sears or Montgomery Ward were unknown. As a consequence, English firms could retain the manageable structure and personal flavor of the past, an orientation evocative of the national commitment to presence on the stage. Even when the British started to catch up, after World War I, the major corporate dynasties developed in less advanced industries like food and toiletries. Manufacturers in these "pre-industrial" areas—Peak Frean in biscuits, Lever Brothers in soap, Cadbury in chocolates—prospered without embracing the multidivisional format.[25] The family concern continued to be the standard type of enterprise, with founders and their heirs exercising control over daily decision-making. In contrast to the American formula, Chandler writes, "The owners managed and the managers owned."[26]

A retrogressive spirit infused this arrangement. Nepotism, anathema to depersonalized administrative corporations, throve in English companies. Managers, taking their cue from above, internalized a "gentlemanly" ideal that laid stress on qualities like manners, education, speech, and style. Long-term investment and risk-taking were less prized than the guarantee of a stable income for the family owners.[27] English businesses had been the pioneers of the first industrial revolution, but, hampered by anti-industrial tendencies, they not surprisingly fell behind in the second revolution of the fin de siècle—steel, chemicals, electricity, automobiles, and the cinema. They have never regained their lead.

## Populism and "Rural Toryism"
### American Defeat, English Triumph

The retardation of British industry was more than a consequence of "personal capitalism." It was also the product of a set of cultural attitudes militating against abstractness and modernization. The deviation from the American philosophy has been summarized this way: the British saw the machine as the enemy of the garden, an intruder in their "green and pleasant land," whereas Americans were receptive to "the machine *in* the garden," perceiving technology as a largely beneficent force that would develop and improve the natural setting.[28] This ideological breach between the two peoples was replayed in the performing arts. The theater fed into English mistrust of industrialism; the movies, a mechanical betterment of nature in their own right, bolstered America's culture of enterprise.

Even as they transformed their nation into "the workshop of the world," Britain's entrepreneurs adopted the outlook of the landed aristocracy. Their goals became those of the ruling class they blended into without overthrowing: owning an estate far from the metropolis, cherishing the countryside for itself and not for profit, following leisured pursuits. The England of their desires was "Old Rural England," with the accents on both the rural and the old, and with a corresponding antipathy to the urban rat-race and the rage for modernizing changes. Dickens, Hardy, Austen, Forster, and other ornaments of the English canon subscribed to this worldview, but by a strange irony one of the most eloquent voices of agrarian nostalgia was an American, Washington Irving. His *Sketch Book of Geoffrey Crayon, Gent.* (1819–20), written when Britain was at the cutting edge of economic dynamism, extolled sleepy village life over commercial bustle. (Irving's Anglophile pieces are unread today in his homeland, being too feudal and antiquarian for American tastes.)

When agricultural capitalism lost preeminence among the English, it was not so much manufacturing that bolted out of the pack as it was the City of London, with its commercial and financial monopolies. Indeed, "workshop of the world" may be a less accurate designation than global "counting house." Banking magnates enjoyed far greater influence and prestige than factory owners. By 1850 or so, they had established London as carrier of the world's trade and dominant player in international exchange. And London firms tended to be considerably more gentrified than industrial companies: they constituted "an extended network of personal contacts based on mutual trust and concepts of honour."[29] Bankers could ally with the landed elite because they too were rentiers living off their holdings. Mostly investments overseas, in their case: they financed those American railroads. Like their brethren elsewhere, English bankers dealt in intangibles like credit and bank notes, but they required a rock-solid foundation for their currency. They found it, as we shall see, in the commodity of gold. London became the century-long defender of sterling, sworn foe of defection from specie and other New World monetary derangements.

It would be hard to overestimate the longevity of anti-industrial sentiment among the English. Fully a hundred and sixty years after Irving's rural panegyrics, Margaret Thatcher made that ideological constellation the target of her campaign for power. Unabashedly pro-capitalist and pro-American, Thatcher promised to rouse the British from their economic slumber; her program called for a thoroughgoing repudiation of the gentlemanly mystique. Not by accident did she take aim at the subsidized theater as well. Thatcher had no need of cultural criticism to grasp the institution's political bias; the stage, beneficiary of government funding (and thus a client of the welfare state), was critical of America, of the movies, and of industrial capitalism.[30]

The overseas variant of British provincialism was the Populist revolt that sought in vain to reverse the growth of incorporated America. Populism combined communitarian and democratic elements with a backward-looking hostility to modern industrialization. Although the agrarian movement championed farmers and the working class against exploitative capital, Teddy Roosevelt was not altogether wrong to denounce it as "rural toryism."[31] Populists shared with the British landed gentry a suspicion of mechanization, and while Americans went further in anti-urbanism, the two groups thought as one in deploring the nonindigenous peoples who settled in cities, such as Eastern European Jews (shortly to flock to Hollywood and to corner the movies, a cultural enterprise looked down upon as vulgar by traditional elites). Agrarians on both sides of the Atlantic, but especially those in the American South and West, felt menaced by the regime of impersonality, the domination of the market system by fictitious legal entities. They much preferred concrete realities like land, crops, and hard currency. (Specie itself, of course, is a kind of fiction or convention. But monetary naturalists cherished metallic coins as real entities with intrinsic worth.)

English "rural tories" have left an indelible mark on modern Britain; American Populists suffered political and cultural disaster. Fusion with the Democrats in 1896 led to the nomination for the presidency of William Jennings Bryan, a Nebraskan who supported free and unlimited coinage of silver. Bryan was also picked to carry the Democratic Party's banner in 1900 and 1908. In all three elections, pro-business Republicans (McKinley twice, and then Taft) scored impressive victories. Buoyed by electoral invincibility, the values of corporate capitalism came to define American society as a whole.[32]

With poetic license, one might describe the movies and the theater as, respectively, "industrial" and "Populist." The drama, as the most English of the arts, is also the most "agrarian." Not that the stage is rustic in its location. Plays are best nurtured by metropolitan soil, invariably reaching their fullest growth in the urban centers where talent, financial backers, and audiences congregate. But this resistance to diffusion and standardization underscores the medium's ontological conservatism. For all its illusoriness, the theater has an affinity with land and physical forms of wealth. It trafficks not just in representations but also in the "thing-in-itself." Actors on the stage pretend to be somebody else, but even as they impersonate another man or woman, they remain flesh-and-blood human beings, real and fully present to the audience. As for the inanimate objects on the set, they are more concrete, more "atavistic," than any thing described in a novel or pictured on the screen. Unlike the *Pequod* in *Moby-Dick* (1851), which is a word and not a ship, and unlike the gun in Al Pacino's hand in *The Godfather* (1972), which is an image on celluloid and not a .32 revolver, sign and signified in the theater can be and often are identical. Although there may be painted scenery on the backdrop, that pitcher of water on the kitchen table literally *is* a pitcher of water, just as the table is a table. Things on the stage exist as what they are. They don't stand for absent objects.

Against this compatibility of the theater and the rural vision can be set the bond of the cinema with industrial capitalism. Populism's rout at the polls occurred simultaneously with the entrance into popular culture of moving pictures. The studios making those pictures were quick to embrace the forms and methods of advanced capitalist enterprise. The artisanal cameraman-writer-director typified by Edwin S. Porter or the early Thomas Ince evolved into a corporate manager overseeing assembly-line production based on the systematic division of labor. Ince, an ardent disciple of Frederick Taylor's scientific management, took decisive steps toward separating conception from execution in film-making. At Inceville, his studio complex in Santa Monica (an analogue to the railroad sleeping car magnate George M. Pullman's corporate town of Pullman near Chicago), Ince assumed total control over thinking processes by devising a shot-by-shot blueprint called a continuity script. Actors, directors, cameramen, fashion designers, and other workers were expected to carry out his detailed instructions without modification. The Inceville facilities churned out standardized product with the efficiency of a well-run factory:

> With preparation laid out in detail from finished photoplays to the last prop, superintended by Mr. Ince himself, far in advance of the action, each of the numerous directors on the job at Santa Ynez canyon is given his working script three weeks ahead of time. . . . Filled with the theme and action, he goes out and, with the cogs of the big Ince machine oiled to the smallest gear and the entire plant running as smoothly as an automobile in the hands of a saleman, the picture travels from the beginning to end without delays.[33]

The Hollywood studio system organized in the twenties and thirties built upon Ince's legacy. The five majors brought motion pictures fully into line with the latest practices of monopoly capitalism. RKO, Warner Brothers, Paramount, Twentieth Century-Fox, and MGM all grew into multimillion dollar companies with their securities traded on the New York Stock Exchange. By 1926, more than sixty thousand individuals owned shares in the movie business, an industry with an annual intake in the United States alone of three quarters of a billion dollars. Structurally, the studios had become vertically integrated trusts little different from those targets of Populist wrath, the railroad and steel combinations. Production, distribution, and exhibition activities were all concentrated under a single corporate roof. The studios manufactured films, delivered them to cities nationwide, and exhibited them in theater chains they owned and operated. Antitrust suits brought against the theater circuits eventually forced the majors to divorce themselves from exhibition in the late 1940s.[34]

Today, of course, motion picture companies are once again part of conglomerates, new media titans whose reach encompasses far more than cinematic entertainment. Disney/Capital Cities not only owns a half dozen studios—among them Walt Disney Pictures, Hollywood Pictures, Touchstone Pictures, and Miramax—it has holdings in radio and television stations, professional sports teams, magazines, newspapers, theme parks, resorts, record companies, cable networks, home video, and mail-order toys. A century after its birth, the movie business, that latecomer to corporate America, has jumped the queue and now occupies the front position in the race to multinational monopoly.

Thus organizational history. As for performance, here, too, the division of labor, the basic principle of post-agricultural society, has insinuated itself into the very core of moviemaking. The dramatic actor plays his or her own role on stage for the duration of the performance. The cinema makes use of doubles and stunt men and women, who specialize in hazardous actions and may spell the stars for long periods on the screen. Film actors may even have "interchangeable" parts like mass-produced goods. Their voices might be dubbed for songs. Other, younger persons, with more shapely figures, or more muscular arms and legs, might stand in for them during nude scenes. And like the worker on an assembly line, the movie actor—for that matter, everybody involved in the production of a film—will have only a provisional sense of how the pieces fit together. The final product, like an automobile or refrigerator, will emerge in the cutting room well after the individual performer has completed his or her particular task.

Those in a state of ignorance include the author. After delivering the script, the writer's part in most filmmaking has effectively ended. Unlike a playwright, who may continue to collaborate with the director and actors until opening night, the writer of a movie is generally excluded from the production process, not even allowed, as Gore Vidal has complained, "to attend the first reading or, in any way ever again, see to his script."[35] Some scenarists do have access to the set, but their control over the resulting picture is sharply limited. John Gregory Dunne, who along with his wife Joan Didion wrote the screenplay for *Up Close and Personal* (1996), added and cut dialogue as the film was shot, but decisions about what to keep or drop rested with the director. Disney executives had totally reconceived the plot of Dunne and Didion's screenplay, reducing their position to that of "highly paid stenographer[s]."[36]

Dozens of writers might be involved in a single picture. Rewrite teams may be brought in to make changes without the original scenarist's knowledge or approval. The subdivision of labor might apply to the composition of gags or love scenes or action sequences. Specialists might have had responsibility for those areas all along. And in the studio days, the writer had to clock in and answer to a "timer," whose job was to calculate the precise running time of the script. A factory hand at General Motors arguably had more in common with a scriptwriter at Columbia or Paramount than did a novelist or playwright.[37]

As their very name indicates, the movies fetishize mobility and circulation, the trademarks of the modern industrial economy. Cinematic special effects require, and often put on display, the advanced technologies produced by that economy (like computer-generated images), for which neither the stage nor small-scale agriculture has much need. The special-effects firm founded by George Lucas, of *Star Wars* (1979—) fame, is the aptly named *Industrial* Light and Magic. And the cinema sides with corporate capitalism against agrarian solidity by substituting immaterial representations for material realities. Signs on the screen, unlike objects in nature, are not unified with their referents. They resemble securities and paper currency in being the traces of something missing.

As remarked previously, the models for the American managerial revolution were the railroads and telegraph systems, advanced capitalist solutions to the forbidding size of the continent. These trailblazing industries anticipated the cinema in two key respects. First, they dealt in services or experiences rather than goods per se, providing consumers, not with material commodities, but with reliable rapid conveyance and with the ability to communicate across great distances. And second, they brought far-away places within the purview of those consumers and enabled them to have the sensation of listening to absent persons. Films consummated as vicarious entertainment the miracles of rail and wire, empowering the stationary viewer-auditor to transcend space and time through mechanically generated spectacle.

A further connection between the movies and the railroad in particular needs to be noted briefly here, as the topic will engage us later. The great transcontinental trunk lines that spurred westward settlement were forerunners of Hollywood in that they inherited, as Nell Painter has said, "the resonance of . . . Manifest Destiny."[38]

It should be pointed out, finally, that the cultural/ideological affiliations scouted in this section have outlived the clash between Populism and the trusts. Well into the twentieth century, pro-theater advocates on both sides of the Atlantic have exalted the preindustrial or "handicraft aspect" of the stage. They have contrasted the drama's auratic values with the mass-produced cinema, which is held to be representative of a "machined and standardized" civilization. The quoted phrases come from one such spokesman, the American playwright Arthur Miller, a latter-day populist (or at least a well-known critic of corporate capitalism). For Miller, spending an evening at the drama is a ceremonial and all-consuming experience that demands exertion from the playgoer; it is like attending church or entering a workshop. "I have never known the smell of sweat in a movie house. I have known it in the theater— and they [sic] are also air-conditioned." Like goods wrought by hand, each theatrical performance has a singularity, "a crap-shooting chanciness," that can never be duplicated at the cineplex. Theater buffs "insist that the unexpected . . . must survive"; moviegoers, in Miller's view of them, are content with the formulaic, the industrial, the commodified.[39]

## Money

NOTHING GOLD CAN STAY

*Nature's first green is gold,*
*Her hardest hue to hold.*
*Her early leaf's a flower;*
*But only so an hour.*
*Then leaf subsides to leaf.*
*So Eden sank to grief,*
*So dawn goes down to day.*
*Nothing gold can stay.*

—

ROBERT FROST (1923)

The attraction between the moving pictures and paper currency is more than a matter of their likeness as insubstantial signs. Their congeniality is rooted in national history. Stretching back to the colonial era, few peoples have been more prone to monetary experimentation than Americans. The land of Thomas Edison and D. W. Griffith and Woody Allen was once the world's paper money capital; and the United States has reclaimed that title in the twentieth century, as it has *become* the capital of cinematic production. By the same token—and *token* is an apposite word here—the British have always shown a flair for sound money and the theater. As a bellwether in both fields in the nineteenth century—the age of gold in international finance but in America no more than "the Gilded Age"—the British have seen the movies depose the drama as popular amusement just as precious metal has given ground to the dollar. "Sterling" and the theater, proud and tangible guardians of England's greatness, have tumbled from their heights together.

A convenient date to begin with would be 1694, the year the Bank of England was established. The "Old Lady of Threadneedle Street," as the Bank came to be known, gained a reputation for promptly redeeming notes in hard coin. But the discussion could just as logically fix on

1690 as its starting point: in that year the Massachusetts Bay Colony solved its chronic cash shortage by authorizing the first issue of paper money in the British Empire. Whitehall tolerated this breach of fiscal probity for half a century before running out of patience. In 1751 Parliament forbade New England further issues of paper, and in 1764 the rest of the colonies came under the ban. Emblematic events: while the British have planted themselves foursquare behind a conservative currency that was "as good as gold," Americans have appreciated the benefits of the inflationary spiral caused by plentiful money.[40]

Britain erected its empire on bullion. From 1816, the end of the Napoleonic Wars, to the outbreak of World War I, altogether almost a century, the island kingdom was on the gold standard. Not only did international trade require payment in gold—or commodity money, as Karl Polanyi has called it—but anyone could exchange a pound note for specie in London, converting his or her "token money" (Polanyi again) into the yellow metal. This absolute convertibility meant, in effect, that Britain had a monetary system predicated on things and not symbols. The very nomenclature of English currency conveys a fealty to the weighty and concrete: the fundamental unit is the "pound" or the "pound sterling" (originally referring to sixteen ounces of silver). To this day, tellers in Lloyd's Bank of London still use small round weights instead of counting machines to determine the worth of specific quantities of coins. And the word *sterling* has entered common usage as a synonym for excellent or authentic; according to the *Concise Oxford Dictionary*, it signifies anything "that is what it seems to be."[41]

The gold standard provided special benefits to the British as an imperial, class-stratified, and creditor nation. Because gold, as a commodity, existed in finite supply, dependence on it had deflationary effects, and the lender would almost always be paid back in money worth more than the money loaned out. Deflation, invariably a policy favoring the well-to-do, was a kind of monetary analogue to the costly and exclusive theater. Scarcity defined both; and both kept the riff-raff in their place. Expensive money made borrowing difficult and limited social mobility. Innumerable discontented citizens who were denied opportunity opted for geographic change over poverty. They pulled up stakes for the New World or the colonies.

Britain's overseas empire ensured London a measure of control over the world's available gold. South Africa, a major source of the precious ore, flew the Union Jack until 1910. (The Boer War of 1899–1902 was fought precisely to determine control of South Africa's mines.) The British forced India, their largest colony, to remain on the silver standard so that in trading with the mother country gold would flow from Delhi to London and not the other way around.

Commodity money, to many Englishmen, was natural because it answered to the laws of supply and demand. Token money, lacking a metallic anchor, was arbitrary and unreal—so how could a stable economy *not* be based on gold? But even English naturalism couldn't withstand the economic shock of global warfare in 1914. In that year—a year before *The Birth of a Nation*, and when American motion pictures were already inundating the English market (with a share of 60 percent)— Whitehall suspended redemption in specie. Gold's prestige as the international totem had effectively ended. Ten years later Winston Churchill, then Chancellor of the Exchequer, restored payment in bullion, but the only noteworthy consequences were increased unemployment and the general strike of 1926. Britain went off the gold standard for good in 1931. Thereafter the dollar, a piece of paper with nothing behind it save the might of the United States, would be the world's monetary flagship, a complement to the domination of mass culture by the weightless moving image.

Americans had manifold reasons to view monetary matters less dogmatically than their erstwhile rulers. A New World hinterland, with a dearth of capital, was not likely to share the metropole's attachment to a limited resource like gold. The Continental Congress had to issue paper in almost boundless amounts to finance the American Revolution, and the young nation came into being, as John Kenneth Galbraith has put it, "on a full tide not of inflation but of hyperinflation."[42] But it was the last third of the nineteenth century that truly defined the Republic's difference from Britain, with the agitation over silver in the 1890s dramatizing the cultural gap. This statement might seem counterfactual. Was it not the case that "free silver," the motto of the Bryanite Democrats, went down to defeat along with the rest of the agrarian program? And did not Washington adopt the gold standard in

1900, ending a century of bimetallism and officially committing the country to monetary alliance with John Bull?

To Populists themselves, certainly, the decade signaled the unholy union of Wall Street with Lombard Street. William H. Harvey, author of the monetary tract, *Coin's Financial School* (1894), lumped English bankers with the Jewish House of Rothschild as persecutors of the American working man and peppered his text with cartoons depicting the British lion preying on Uncle Sam. But like Populists generally, Harvey favored hard money—the white ore in this instance—and insisted that paper had to be redeemable in coin. His pro-silver fanaticism was not the opposite but the mirror image of the British passion for gold; and his anti-Semitism, or rather the variant of it excoriating poor Jews instead of rich ones, fell on more sympathetic ears in turn-of-the-century London than in New York.

While gold's victory over silver at the polls may have pleased Anglophiles, the real winners were the modernizers. The forces of nativist concreteness had lost. The United States was to approximate Great Britain only by outstripping her as both imperial and monetary powerhouse. Silver's repudiation occurred alongside and paralleled the transition in America from personal to managerial capitalism. Far from representing an apostasy to deflation, anti-Populism reaffirmed the country's commitment to a capacious and, as time was to prove, a purely figurative currency. Gold triumphed in part because discoveries in South Africa and the Klondike, simultaneous with the end of the 1893–1896 depression, sparked an inflationary rise in prices. Prosperity and plentiful money eased the passage of the Gold Standard Act. Governmental gold reserves soared, and by the time Britain abandoned convertiblity in 1914, the United States boasted a surplus of the yellow metal. This no doubt reassured goldbugs, but the trove's utility was not destined to last. The dollar, which American citizens couldn't exchange for gold anyway, was on the road to becoming as disembodied as the cinematic apparition. The land that had astonished London with its monetary laxness was soon to abjure the specie foundation of money altogether.

The uncoupling occurred in three stages. Its economy reeling from the Great Depression, the United States jettisoned the gold standard in

1933. Bullion was no longer necessary for international trade; the country conducted its business in paper. Then in 1944, with Allied success in World War II assured, representatives of the victorious nations assembled at Bretton Woods, New Hampshire, to establish the International Monetary Fund (IMF) and the World Bank as the props of postwar recovery. The objective was to secure the stability of the gold standard without dependence on gold; in reality, the unofficial global currency was the dollar. The Bretton Woods agreement was itself scrapped in 1971, marking the final abandonment of monetary naturalism.[43] Token money in the form of U.S. greenbacks circulated worldwide, as free-floating and as welcome as the projected likeness of Paul Newman or Goldie Hawn. And despite brief usurpations by the deutsch mark and the Japanese yen, the dollar has reigned as the paper standard of the twentieth century.

The British have not, however, altogether forsaken their devotion to a hard or strong currency. Since the 1920s, successive governments have "defended" sterling as somehow symbolic of national prestige. The result, as any visitor to the United Kingdom knows, is an extravagantly overvalued pound (not to mention guaranteed trade deficits and the steady diminution of British industry, unable to sell its overpriced products abroad).[44] What a dollar buys in the United States, a pound purchases in England; but on the international currency markets, the same dollar buys only a fraction of a pound. The American tourist has had to shell out anywhere from $1.50 to $1.80 to obtain approximately one dollar's worth of goods. This makes the London theater's relative cheapness all the more of a bargain. Sterling may no longer be as solid as gold, but it continues to put up a good show of being a more substantial currency than the greenback.

A note has to be added about a forward-looking pair of British capitalists who dissented from the national enthusiasm for hard coin. Heads of a merchant banking concern, the Ostrer brothers deserve mention in any discussion of filmmaking and monetary policy. English as they were, the two might be thought of as Americans manqué. They were Jewish, as were of course the moving spirits of Hollywood. The Ostrers had a prime role in developing one of the two major London studios, Gaumont-British, a fully vertically integrated firm designed to meet the challenge of American competition. One brother in particular, Isidore, stands out for his prescience about mass culture: he also invested in radio stations, early television, and the popular press. And he was a good friend of John Maynard Keynes, whose ideas on economic reform he adapted in composing his own attack on British conservatism, aptly titled *The Conquest of Gold* (1932).[45]

This book, which Ostrer dedicated "To Humanity," coheres around a single theme: the need to get money into movement or circulation. The idea must have seemed inescapable to a man involved in moving pictures. Ostrer rails against the gold standard and its requirement of convertibility on demand: the effects being deflationary, people are inclined to leave their money on deposit in banks rather than spending it to stimulate the economy. To force money into use, Ostrer proposes the radical step of charging *depositors* interest for the socially harmful practice of secreting away their resources. He further suggests the creation of a World Bank and the conversion of gold from a currency anchor into a kind of bookkeeping token for recording transactions between nations. But the retention of the "red metal" (as he calls gold) in international finance is merely a concession to British prejudice, Ostrer admits. Gold is an "asset of no real usefulness" and might be dispensed with altogether, to be replaced by "theoretical Alphas," imaginary signs which would track commercial exchanges and have behind them only "the guarantees of the State itself."[46]

Ostrer's shrewd little treatise anticipates the IMF, the World Bank, and the emergence of the post–gold standard dollar as the global medium of exchange. Driving its disaffection from gold is the same modernizing impulse of disembodiment that turned this English Jew into a pathbreaking filmmaker and a precursor of Robert Maxwell and Rupert Murdoch. But Ostrer, a patriot who is supposed to have offered to sell Gaumont-British to the government, would not have relished the irony that history made of his title: as it turned out, *The Conquest of Gold* was coterminous with the conquest of Britain by the United States as world imperium and of live entertainment by the intangible circulating image.

## Wealth

Money has a direct as well as a symbolic relation to filmmaking. For all sterling's elitist pretensions, there have never been quite enough pounds in circulation to bankroll a plausible threat to Hollywood. Britain's comparative *lack* of money, its indigence vis-à-vis America since World War I, has dampened cinematic ambition for the simple reason that motion pictures are the most costly art form ever devised. The United States, as the richest society on earth, has been the almost inevitable capital (no pun intended) of the industry, the one nation consistently able to afford the expense of financing films. Just as no single country can equal the United States in the production of passenger planes, for example, so at forty million dollars apiece—the average price of a Hollywood picture in the 1990s—the American cinema can outspend, outdistribute, and outdraw all competitors. (The average figure, which includes promotional and advertising costs, climbed to $60 million in 1996.)[47]

An unfortunate corollary of this great wealth has been the monopolization of cultural agency. For enormous expenses create equally enormous pressures. The demand in Hollywood to generate global hits in order to recoup multimillion dollar budgets—the so-called blockbuster mentality—has had the result of appropriating more and more power into fewer and fewer hands. Shrinking participation, the norm on the business end as well as in the movie house, infiltrates the culture as a whole. The theater, where expenses are far less, has the opposite effect of encouraging widespread involvement. Many more plays get performed than films released, and many more individuals, in toto, take part in the processes of decision-making, designing sets, acting, directing, and stage-managing. Is it too much to suggest that, owing to the prestige of the movies, Americans are forsaking the habit of aesthetic performance? For its size, the United States lags well behind England in amateur involvement in (the admittedly class-stratified arts of) music, drama, and the dance.

## Climate

The American cinema got its start on the East Coast. Edison's work-shop was located in West Orange, New Jersey, and there he built the first studio, named the Black Maria, from which he shipped footage to Kinetoscope parlors throughout the country. (To cope with the Northeast's unpredictable skies, the Black Maria came equipped with wheels so that it could rotate to catch the sun's rays.) Griffith worked for Biograph, which was housed in a brownstone on East Fourteenth Street in New York, and later he made pictures in the Westchester suburb of Mamaroneck. Paramount was still operating a studio complex on Long Island in the 1920s.

But the exodus to Hollywood had already begun, and the explana-tion for the move was a simple one: better climate. Rain and snow, impediments to filming scenes outside the studio, fell regularly along the Atlantic seaboard but seldom troubled the South or far West. Bright skies were a doubly urgent necessity in the medium's youth because primitive motion-picture stock couldn't capture clear images with any-thing less than the strongest light.[48] Early directors in search of sunny locales scouted New Mexico, Arizona, Jacksonville (Fla.), and New Orleans before converging on Los Angeles as the most reliable site for production. Spared the vagaries of weather, studios could schedule year-round shooting, a gain in economy as well as a convenience, since actors and cameramen no longer had to be paid to wait for the horizon to clear.

To state the matter as bluntly as possible, England lacks the neces-sary climate to have established a bustling movie industry. (The handi-cap is no longer so disabling, with improved film stock and the global-izing of production.) Nowhere on the island, and emphatically not in London, does one see the consistently sunny skies that in southern California permitted outdoor filming an average of 320 days in a year. Grayness, fog, drizzle, and poor light are hardly ideal conditions for a medium that achieves its best results in the open air. Drama has suited the English better because, even when the mise-en-scène is a storm-rav-aged heath or a metropolitan street, the action occurs indoors, within the four walls of the theater. (That mid-August downpour leaking onto the King's Head stage says as much about why the cinema shunned London as it does about the informality of the theater.) English films, with some notable exceptions, incline to interior settings for the same reason: directors couldn't count on enough decent weather to be sure of meeting their deadlines.

Which is to say that an insufficiency of natural resources, once the impetus to English industrial progress, has cramped the kingdom's cinematic development—in this case, a scarcity of sunshine.

### Abundance and Scarcity

Hollywood filmmakers love to dazzle viewers with images of plenty. In no other nation's cinema is conspicuous consumption so unalloyed a good. Palatial homes stocked with every imaginable gadget, chauffeur-driven limosines equipped with bars and televisions, Olympic-sized swimming pools—the list could be extended indefinitely. But the bounty on display is not merely, perhaps not even principally, of human manufacture. American nature in all its rich diversity fills the screen as well. The lavishness of the continent—profuse not only in arable soil, minerals, oil, timber, and other resources but also in topographical marvels unknown in Great Britain—is a cinematic cliché promising the endless satisfaction of desire.49

English nature, on the other hand, seems to murmur of more moderate pleasures. True it is that the island kingdom boasts its own geographic diversity. Present-day visitors fan out to the Lake District, the Peak District, the Cotswolds, Scotland, and Wales. In the nineteenth century, ample waterways and stores of coal powered the industrial revolution. And the wealth of the sea has been a constant. But compared to the continental cornucopia of the United States, Britain's physical assets seem more pinched than prodigal. The comparative dearth of resources may help to explain both the country's head start in industrialization and its swift ascent to imperial power. (The strength of the British nation-state, protected by geographic insularity, was a factor as well.) Without adequate natural gifts to supply its people's wants, Britain compensated by seizing more fecund territory elsewhere and by plunging into the production of finished goods. India and Kenya had those missing mountain ranges, and fine china could be exchanged for American tobacco.

Such things affect temperament and the arts. Americans are famous (and usually admired) for their expansiveness and generosity. They are disliked for their gluttony and sense of entitlement. British reserve and ability to make do ("muddling through") are legendary.[50] (Anyone who has sampled the native English cuisine might want to amend that to "ability to do without.") The cinema and the stage might be described as possessing analogous dispositions. While no one would call the commercial theater abstemious, in relation to the movies plays are modest consumers of resources. They don't require anything like the same outlay of financial, technological, and staff support. The most exorbitant West End productions can cost as much as two or three million pounds; but Hollywood spectaculars regularly overrun budgets of a hundred million dollars. The movies are insatiable in their appetite for goods and money. Self-denial is foreign to them. Whereas plays of necessity observe formal rules, doggedly staying within the constraints of time and space, movies exuberantly bid defiance to the unities of dramatic convention. But the real cultural impact of the differing provisions of nature can be seen in the character of the movies themselves. American cinematic spontaneity and the theater-like quality of English film are inextricable from the frugality or liberality of geographic endowment.

Ownership of plentiful resources obviously lessens inhibition about expending them. If the supply, say, of thickly forested land appears to be inexhaustible, there will be little motivation to exercise restraint in building houses of wood. With respect to the movies, this axiom applies to any number of elements but to none more basic than reels of film. Here as elsewhere the United States cinema has enjoyed a sizable advantage over its competitors. Since the 1890s, Eastman Kodak has been the international purveyor of negative. The reasons are two: George Eastman founded his Rochester company's success on his patent for 35 millimeter sprocketed motion picture film. (Perhaps one should add technological ingenuity to the catalogue of American resources, although know-how is an area where the British set the standard.) And second, the United States possessed the ample stores of silver required to manufacture celluloid. By a happy chance, the great silver lodes in the western mining states of Colorado and Nevada were discovered a decade or two before Edison's experiments with the Kinetoscope. By the 1920s, motion pictures were gobbling up more silver annually than the United States Mint; and down to this day of blockbusters and videotape, Kodak remains the world's single largest consumer of the white ore. These two circumstances guaranteed that the raw stock needed for filmmaking—constituting anywhere from 5 to 10 percent of a picture's cost—was cheaper and more readily available in this country than abroad.[51]

Without incentive to economize, Americans threw caution to the winds. They could shoot and reshoot until they got the scenes exactly right. Irving Thalberg, production head at MGM in the twenties, was such a perfectionist that people referred to his studio headquarters as "retake valley." Mistakes in performance or direction were unfortunate but reparable. The pressure on actors to arrive on the set with lines down pat was minimal. Spontaneity ("not acting" or not appearing to act) looked natural on the screen anyway. The "Method" style of acting won adherents among American moviemakers in part because film stock was so abundant. Improvising, trying out different lines or facial expressions or bodily poses, meant being able to run through reams of footage in quest of serendipitous results.

Similar but inverted causes impelled the British cinema toward rehearsals and formal acting. While these emphases had their origins in England's theatrical tradition, their persistence into motion pictures was also owing to the expense and shortage of film. Mistakes being costly, the goal was to hold shootings to a minimum. Movie actors behaved like stage players: they came to the lot with their lines prepared and with the intention of performing their actions correctly the first time, as they would if playing their roles in front of a live audience. From the lighting, through the choreography of physical movements, to the arrangement of objects on the set, everything had to be right before the cameras started to roll. The more impromptu attitude of Hollywood actors and directors would have broken the budget of many an English filmmaker.[52]

How fitting that the cinema should exhibit a bias toward liberality! Plenitude is inscribed in the medium's very nature as a mechanically reproduced art, with a built-in capacity for proliferation. A film can spawn an infinite number of copies. Every dramatic performance is unique, every movie an exact duplicate. Live plays have a one-of-a-kind, artisanal scarcity, screened narratives a manufactured superabundance.

Many copies, but also a multitude of new films: the plethora of American pictures has directly dampened English cinematic output. The sheer number of movies from Hollywood has saturated the English market during this century. An indigenous film industry—not to mention the British public's appetite for home-grown product—has been slow to materialize in the face of so much formidable competition. This transatlantic flow of domination reverses the history of an earlier cultural artifact, the novel. Americans produced little fiction of note until the nineteenth century. Among other causes, the delay can be attributed to the flooding of these shores by more accomplished and myriad English authors. Why read *The Power of Sympathy* (1789), an amateurish tale of seduction by the Bostonian William Hill Brown, when *Clarissa* (1748–49) was available at the local bookseller's? Hollywood movies are the belated payback for the novels of Defoe, Fielding, Richardson, and Austen.

A last observation about silver: the specie that Populist orators championed as being more beneficial to economic growth than gold did not convert the fin-de-siècle electorate to their cause, but it did help to secure American preeminence in cinema, and it underwrote the unobtrusive mode of acting that has made Hollywood's stars the biggest in the business.

## Individualism

It is not suprising that America's open spaces should foster a partiality for individualism and solitude. The frontiersman heading West made a choice, at least initially, for isolation over community. His odyssey, taking him far from the nearest neighbor, weakened his ties to others. He was alone, and he had no one to rely on but himself.

The impulse that begot Daniel Boones and Natty Bumppos, and was nourished by the presence of cheap land, drew support from ideological sources as well, such as the right of every person, as enshrined in the Declaration of Independence, to pursue his or her happiness. The Frenchman Alexis de Tocqueville regarded equality, another principle set forth in the Declaration, as the root of American atomization: it diminished dependence and stoked the fires of competitiveness. Tocqueville has left an unsurpassed account of the democratic penchant to go it alone. "Individualism," he stated in 1835,

> is a mature and calm feeling, which disposes each member of the community to sever himself from the mass of his fellows and to draw apart with his family and his friends, so that after he has formed a little circle of his own, he willingly leaves society at large to itself.[53]

Another French student of United States culture, this time writing in the twentieth century, has corroborated Tocqueville's analysis. The social anthropologist Raymonde Carroll concludes that for the French (and, one might speculate, for other Europeans too), "I exist in a network." For the American, "I exist outside all networks."[54]

Sitting inside the dark screening room of a mall multiplex, with no intermission in which to socialize, and staring at a hypnotic block of color, appears to be the antithesis of communal involvement. Yet perhaps one should pause before stigmatizing the cinema as a domain of autistic self-enclosure. It could be asserted against this conclusion that movie houses provide an antidote to the infirmity of privatism. Every time the moviegoer attends a picture show, he or she has to leave home to enter a public setting. Association with others is mandatory, if only to stand in line in order to purchase tickets and candy. And does not the viewer, caught up in the glowing spectacle, step out of his or her narrow absorptions and participate imaginatively in the life of other human beings?

Tocqueville, for one, thought that American individualism found its potential remedy in "the art of association." Because the United States had no aristocratic great men on the European model, able to move mountains with their wealth and influence, citizens had to band together in voluntary groups to accomplish the smallest undertakings. Americans formed assemblages of a thousand kinds, "to give entertainments, to found seminaries, to build inns, to construct churches, to diffuse books, to send missionaries to the antipodes." The movies, it may be, constitute another experiment in democratic association, a voluntary gathering to lure the privatized individual out of "the solitude of his own heart."[55]

Although there are good arguments to be made on both sides of the issue, the preponderance of evidence bears out the movies' isolationism. At times in its history, the cinema has permitted a degree of fellowship more like a club or PTA meeting (or the present-day London theater) than the uninviting multiplex. But such outbreaks of community, which might reasonably be compared to Tocqueville's civic organizations, have invariably succumbed to the medium's reclusive tendencies. In fact, it might be more appropriate to think of the cinema as forming an episode in the century-long deformation of American civil society into something like anonymous collectivity. Movies bring people together, it is true, but the people meet as a crowd or mass of discrete individuals, the overwhelming majority of whom are not only strangers but invisible to each other and who have nothing in common beyond their being in the same physical location at the same time. Further, instead of drawing the spectator into communion with other persons, the story on the screen merely intensifies the isolation of the experience. The filmgoer identifies with the moving but insentient images; the living beings in the nearby seats are forgotten.

If one returns to Poe's "Man of the Crowd," one can see how the union of the anonymous and the collective shapes the sensibility of modernity. The tale's prescience consists as much in its erosion of community as in its vision of acceleration. Poe's narrative is set in the city of London, a preview of the populous future for Americans, and the eponymous protagonist is a type of the modern individual. Hastening to and fro with no destination, he compulsively submerges himself in the crowd. He knows no one and is himself unknowable. Poe describes this mysterious walker as a book that "does not permit itself to be read," and the comparison might be updated: the man of the crowd is a figure of the moviegoer, a seeker at once of anonymity and of the comfort of the multitude.

Jean-Jacques Rousseau thought that attending plays sapped feelings of civic responsibility; he could not foresee how the movies would carry to extreme the theater's passivity and privatization. But it is not necessary to adopt Rousseau's (or Tocquville's) censorious attitude. One might concede that individualism has a cognitive affinity with moviegoing and still find something positive in the supercession of cultural *gemeinschaft* by *gesellschaft*.

Once again, Lindsay's little tome offers an alternative and optimistic reading of the cinema's impersonal conglomeration. Lindsay admits that the audience for film is not a community in the theatrical sense but rather a "crowd" or a "mob." (Mindful of the prevalence of crowd scenes in early cinema, Lindsay speculates that "the mob comes nightly to behold its natural face in the glass.") Rather than lamenting this mass formation, he welcomes it as ensuring the individual an enclave of freedom. He points out that early moviegoers entered picture shows one or two at a time, and at no specified hour. They blended anonymously into the group. Thanks to the protective covering of facelessness, these separate persons were more at liberty to form (and trust) their own opinions: "The newcomers do not, as in Vaudeville, make themselves part of a jocular army. Strictly as individuals they judge the panorama."[56]

So the state of cinematic art represented by the VCR confronts us with a curiosity. In an obvious respect, home viewing amplifies the process of withdrawal from society, confining each individual, to paraphrase Tocqueville, to his or her own little family circle. The movies, which began life as an outgrowth of photography and the stage (among other sources), have devolved into a thoroughly privatized modern version of the "novel," mass entertainment for domestic consumption. But in another respect, the VCR checks the modernist drift toward atomization. It brings us, if not a reawakening of community, at least a respite from crowd-like anonymity. Settled in the familiar environs of home, the viewer watches among family or friends. And home video makes possible again the temporal randomness of primitive moviegoing. The experience is individualistic in the preregulated, predisciplinary sense: one can switch on the machine at any time, free from the clockbound punc-tuality of public attendance.

## Privacy

Still, the home viewer occupies a sequestered space (he or she may be solitary within that space), and there is no doubt that the experience of cinematic spectatorship, particularly in these days of single features and small, warren-like screening rooms, is more privatized than theatergo-ing. This distribution of emphasis corresponds to the greater or lesser importance attached to privacy by American and English culture—at any rate, as a right encoded in law.

The private understood as a legally protected interest is the subject of a growing body of doctrine in American jurisprudence (most famously in *Roe v. Wade*, where the Supreme Court overturned state abortion statutes as violating a constitutional right of privacy), but has no explicit equivalent in English common law. American inception and extension of rules safeguarding privacy evolved alongside the cinema. This should surprise no one because the identical technological advances that brought forth the movies created the anxieties for which the emergent system of laws offered relief.

The opening blow came in 1890 when two Boston lawyers, Samuel D. Warren and Louis D. Brandeis, were so disturbed by the spread of "instantaneous photography" and journalistic sensationalism that they coauthored an essay on "The Right to Privacy" for the *Harvard Law Review*. Prior to this time, images on film had presented no threat to the personal sphere because the camera had to be posed for, usually by sit-ting or standing still for some minutes; the device could catch no one unawares. The new power to capture movement, the requisite condition for motion picture development, exposed "the sacred precincts" of pri-vate life to invasion and permitted the unauthorized abduction of one's likeness.

Warren and Brandeis proposed to fend off these dangers by postu-lating a right "to be let alone" that would have the same legal standing as tangible property. The basis for such a right, the two men argued, could be found in the common law inherited from England. British copyright protections were accorded to unpublished manuscripts and personal letters. Such decisions, on the surface addressed to material possessions, amounted to an indirect acknowledgment of the need to preserve "thoughts, emotions, and sensations" from wrongful intrusion. The judges had recognized the unprecedented dangers to the self arising in a complex commercial civilization. Their object was "in reality not the principle of private property, but that of an inviolate personality."[57]

Warren and Brandeis's reasoning, and the revolution they wrought in American jurisprudence (where their thesis had won the day by 1905), were cognate with the supplanting of the English stage by Hollywood. In a maneuver analogous to film's "improvement" upon the drama, the screen's leaving behind of human beings and three-dimensional sets for insubstantial shadows, they substituted an incorporeal right for the legal protection of "physical things"[58] operative in Britain. They hit upon a kind of legal correlative to the moviegoer's enclosed autonomy, which today reaches its apogee in that domestic domain they were determined to render impregnable. The British theater lover is part of the "jocular army" of a unified audience. The cinematic spectator can enjoy the sensation of being let alone, either by sitting in solitude at the multiplex or by retreating to a private residence. (The very phrase, "the right to be let alone," evokes American individualist ideology in its classical liberal form, as opposed to the British fidelity to communal welfare—much frayed by the Conservative Party's marketeers.)

English common law, cited by Warren and Brandeis as the seed for their theory, declined to adopt the cisatlantic privacy principle. British judges simply do not recognize a general right to be let alone; at best they counterfeit American developments by elaborating copyright or other existing protections. On at least four separate occasions—in 1961, 1967, 1969, and 1970—legislative steps were taken to compensate for the legal omission by considering a privacy statute. But the bills never made it into law, and the 1970 Committee on Privacy set up by Parliament decided not to tamper with the ad hoc approach.[59] Partly as a consequence, governmental supervision of videocassettes extends well beyond the ratings system employed in the United States. The British have their classifications too, but they also enforce censorship in the home by imposing cuts on violent or obscene material before it becomes available for domestic viewing. To Americans (and to many Britons), this invasion of private life smacks of Orwellian Big Brother.[60]

In one other significant regard, it seems logical that a legal right to privacy should have caught on in the United States but not in Great Britain. The emphasis, in the Warren and Brandeis piece, on the sanctity of the individual personality belongs to a democratic culture. Let us concede that American society's inequities militate against self-fulfillment for many of its citizens. Nonetheless, the regime of the "First Person Singular" (as Ralph Waldo Emerson named it), of the theoretically equal democratic subject, has long prevailed in America and prevails in the one-price/one-view movie houses. In Britain, political equality has foundered on hereditary peerage and social class—and, so to speak, on the discrepant prices, and nonfungible views, of the London theater.

## Bodies and the Senses

Not only does the stage require living persons, actual bodies that perspire and fumble lines on occasion, in contrast to the cinema's flawless simulacra, the theater forces upon the spectator a greater awareness of his or her own physical being, of the resources and deficiencies of bodily nature. One reason that the movies can charge a single admission price to viewers who will end up sitting in different sections of the auditorium, some near the screen, others far away, some in the very center ten rows back, others on the periphery, is that all ticket buyers are assumed to enjoy an equally good view of the action. The wonders of technology guarantee equivalence of access. Every inch of the screen is theoretically visible to all, and the dialogue, the sighs, and the murmurs are audible at all points of the theater. (Exceptions of course exist, but one can usually move to another seat if a very tall individual happens to be in one's line of vision. As for the whispering or talking that other spectators sometimes indulge in, it can scarcely compete with the blast of noise coming from the sound track; the volume, if anything, is turned up much too high in most of today's multiplexes.)

The drama, acknowledging uneven human capacity, both natural and social, doesn't presume to be a domain of equality. The Royal Shakespeare Company charges higher prices for better seats; in exchange for more money, it promises a closer or less obstructed vision of the stage and a better chance of hearing every syllable spoken by the actors. The less affluent theatergoer in Row Q, Left, is inescapably conscious of his or her bodily limits: an inability to decipher facial expressions from seventy-five feet away, or to perceive certain gestures from the side, or to understand what the characters are saying when they lower their voices or fail to enunciate distinctly. The prosperous but older viewer, able to afford the best tickets but afflicted with diminished sensory powers, will experience some of the same difficulties. Consciousness of sensory deprivation was still more extreme in the nineteenth century, when people regularly suffered headaches because the brilliant gaslight used to illuminate theaters consumed tremendous amounts of oxygen.[61]

On the other hand, senses unutilized at the movies may be activated at the drama. Theatergoers will be able to smell food cooking on a stove; their eyes may water from smoke drifting into the audience from a murky night scene. And there is the constant danger of an empathetic shiver of embarrassment caused by a performer's forgetting his or her lines, a tremor registered on the body as a blush of discomfort.

In short, the stage is a medium of increased presence for the spectator as well as the performer, owing for the most part to the body's infirmities. Here again the theater allies itself with English naturalism and immediacy, in contrast to the disembodiment and modernism of the movies. The English, blessed with a human-scale natural environment that is more friend than antagonist, tamper far less with bodily irregularities than Americans, who not only lead the field in plastic surgeons but in toiletries, cosmetics, and high-pressure showers. The enforcement of social class in ticket prices is perhaps less telling as an index of national identity than the structural acceptance of human differences, the fact that hierarchies of reception are built into the theatergoing process and submitted to as though they were irrevocable. The birthmark on Katey Kastin's cheek, one might say, is reproduced in the drama's mode of consumption: the ticket holder for a revival of *King Lear*, prevented by distance or age from taking in every important confidence and motion, experiences on his or her own pulses the imperfection, and the inequality, of physical endowment. And no effort is made to eradicate this offense to American values.

"The Spectacles," a tale by Poe (who seems to have written about virtually all facets of cultural consumerism), noted the spectatorial body's weaknesses a hundred and fifty years ago. The tale is narrated by a young man with poor eyesight who falls in love with a "queenly apparition" he observes from a distance at the theater. A marriage is arranged, and the young man discovers to his horror that he has wed his rouged and bewigged great, great grandmother, aged eighty-two. Only then is it revealed that the wedding ceremony has been a hoax, concocted in order to cure the narrator of his vanity for refusing to wear eyeglasses.

The movies are the spectacles of popular entertainment, a prosthetic correction for the disabilities and discriminations of the theater.

## Theme Parks

By common consent, the United States is the originator and natural home of the theme park. No one did more to propagate the institution than Walt Disney, whose Disneyland, located in Anaheim, California, a stone's throw from Hollywood, opened in 1955. Disney's stature as the world's premier animated cartoonist needs little introduction. Along with his brother Roy, he founded a studio in 1924 and won instant fame four years later with *Steamboat Willie*, a short that featured Mickey Mouse and inaugurated the practice of using a single drawing for each motion. Disney Bros. Studio produced the first feature-length cartoon, *Snow White and the Seven Dwarfs*, a decade later, in 1938, and then subsequently perfected the method of combining live actors with cartoon characters.[62]

Disney, who wanted to upgrade the animated short much as Griffith had legitimated the narrative film, entertained similar ambitions for the amusement park. When he originally conceived the idea of Disneyland, he intended to exclude rides like the roller coaster and to ban beer and outdoor hot dog stands, all of which cheapened the tone. (The smells especially offended him.) *His* park was not to resemble some common fairground but to be divided into discrete "lands," each with its own theme. Exotic settings and futuristic fantasies would complement the strategic screening of classic Disney films. The format was a hit and has spawned innumerable imitators. It has also sired three additional Disney parks, the gigantic Walt Disney World near Orlando, Florida, and two foreign operations, Tokyo Disneyland and Euro Disneyland outside Paris.

These theme parks, as befits their etiology, reflect the American/cinematic worldview. They overleap the limitations of space and time, bridging future (Tomorrowland) and past (Frontierland) and transporting the ticket holder through ancient and modern societies. They fetishize verisimilitude, promising that in every pavilion "the attention to historical detail is meticulous."[63] They embrace multinational capitalism. Corporate sponsors of attractions and rides (all "themed" to escape the taint of ordinary amusement parks) include AT&T, IBM, Kodak, General Motors, Delta Airlines, Exxon, General Electric, and United Technologies. No visitor to the parks can miss the United States's imperial insouciance. At World Showcase in Florida (part of Disney World), the globe offers itself compliantly to the American family, whose members can amble past the fabricated landscape, architecture, cuisine, and products of eleven countries. (Euro Disney touched off the same kind of protests against American cultural imperialism that the movies have incited. The Paris venture, initially a financial calamity, has turned the corner and is now a great success.)

If the moving pictures define the archetypal American theme park, the theater was the incubator of the English model. Stratford-upon-Avon, which one enthusiast has dubbed "Shakespeareland," was arguably the first example of the institution, prefiguring Disney's Anaheim site by almost two centuries. In 1768 a group of Stratford townsmen approached David Garrick, considered the age's greatest living actor-manager, with the idea of organizing a Shakespeare Jubilee. Three days of festivities were planned for the following year. Despite relentless wet weather (a condition unknown at the American Disney parks), the celebrations attracted thousands of visitors and nationwide publicity. Events included a Shakespeare pageant, a masquerade ball, and numerous banquets, and Garrick dedicated an amphitheater and a statue of the bard.[64]

Although no plays were performed during the jubilee, Stratford has come to symbolize England's dramatic heritage. As a "theme park," it has its tourist hype and overpriced shops peddling Prince Hamlet gewgaws. But for the most part, the town takes its lead from the theater's communalism and personalized entrepreneurial style. The first Shakespeare Memorial Theater opened in 1879—Americans put up more than half the funds, an augury of the United States's wealth and power—and a festival of plays has been staged annually ever since. There are now three active theaters, the Main House, the Swan, and The Other House, and the season, once covering just a few weeks, runs for more than six months a year, from March to October.

In 1891 Parliament passed a Trust Act to purchase the buildings and other properties connected with Shakespeare. His birthplace and two residences belonging to his descendants, Nash's House and Hall's Croft, plus Anne Hathaway's cottage in nearby Shottery and the home of his mother, Mary Arden, in Wilmcote, all became national memorials. Today they belong to the English people as a whole.

At Disneyland tourists are not allowed to take photographs without prior approval. The buildings and landscape have been copyrighted by the corporation. Unauthorized images not belonging to Disney/Capital Cities are confiscated.

## Jews

Jews have been among the principal architects of the movie industry, and no country save Israel has been as welcoming to them as the United States. Almost without exception the Jewish moguls or their parents emigrated from Eastern Europe. Neal Gabler, author of the best study of these men, lists their places of origin: Adolph Zukor, born in Hungary;

William Fox, the child of recent Hungarian immigrants; Carl Laemmle, born in Germany; the Warner brothers, four sons of a Polish peddler; Harry Cohn, whose father was a German tailor; and Louis B. Mayer, born in Russia to parents who soon fled to the New World.[65]

Jewish visibility remains high in the film business today, as illustrated by the successes of Steven Spielberg, Michael Eisner, Sherry Lansing, Dustin Hoffman, Woody Allen, Bette Midler, Richard Dreyfuss, Barry Levinson, and numerous others.

The founding generation made the movies into "America's new civic religion," in Gabler's phrase, and in the process transformed themselves into uncritical celebrants of their adopted homeland. They effectively shed their Judaism in their urgency to assimilate. If this was a Faustian bargain, it was one that the founders were more than willing to undertake. Hollywood rewarded them with riches and power, and their identification with the United States was so thoroughgoing that one of them, Louis B. Mayer, professing not to remember his Russian birthdate, claimed to have been born on the Fourth of July.[66] (Henry David Thoreau began his experiment in the woods on the same day, according to *Walden* [1854], and D. W. Griffith picked the festive occasion to start shooting *The Birth of a Nation* [1915]. Of the three, only Thoreau meant the date, emblem of fresh beginnings, to imply a criticism of extant American society.)

Not that the Zukors and Cohns were spared prejudice on these shores; American hospitality definitely had its limits. The Johnson-Reed Act of 1924 curtailing immigration was aimed at Jews as well as other Eastern and Southern Europeans; and admission quotas went unfilled in the Nazi era because of obstacles erected by nativists. But the American lapses look mild when compared to the English record. Expelled from England in 1290 as religious aliens, the Jews had been readmitted in the seventeenth century without full civil rights; two centuries later, they were still ineligible for university degrees and barred from holding public office. (It was possible for Benjamin Disraeli to become prime minister, but only because he had converted as a boy.)[67]

In the great migration of peoples from Eastern Europe between 1880 and World War I, some two million Jews deserted Russia, Poland, and Rumania; scarcely one-tenth chose Britain as their destination.

Those who did encountered active hostility. Proposals to restrict "pauper foreign immigrants," as the current phrase had it, were introduced into Parliament as early as the 1880s. In 1894, just around the time the movies were being invented, an Aliens Bill got a receptive hearing from the House of Lords; a later bill became law in 1905, requiring new arrivals to show proof of ability to support themselves and their dependents. Thus did Britain, civilized nerve center of the drama and nineteenth-century bulwark of political liberalism, become one of the first nations in the West to pass legislation against the influx of Jewish foreigners.[68]

## Things or the Reign of Commodities

In the United States, the reign of the market has been more complete than elsewhere, and with it the penetration of all aspects of life by the commodity form. Film Americanizes in that it gives sovereignty to the world of things. Most obviously, the movies raise to a heightened pitch that visual representation of material objects that John Berger has described, in his study of Western painting, as converting seeing into an act of possession—possession understood as being potential as well as actual. Around the time of the Renaissance, according to Berger, oil painting began to exhibit to the viewer a vision of what he or she might own: not only the canvas itself but the physical universe as objects or merchandise available for purchase, objects in all their tangibility, texture, and color: buildings, animals, weapons, clothes, art works, lobsters, furniture.[69]

Cinema differs from painting in that it cannot be owned or touched—although videocassettes have in a measure overcome the incorporealness of film—and in its appeal to the spectator not as present owner but as future consumer. But the movies represent an undeniable extension of painting's materialism in the greater vividness and immediacy with which they render the world. What painting can hope to compete with the screen in celebrating the ownership of things? What stationary image in pigment can approach the cinema's ability to dazzle us with the speed and romance of a new automobile?

More subtly, the movies bestow upon physical objects a prominence in storytelling that far exceeds their position in other narrative arts. Not even the novel, and least of all the theater, can match film's foregrounding of the inanimate. In theater, actors and their words dominate the mise-en-scène; in the cinematic cosmos, matter rivals Hamlet in power of speech, and things can equal or overshadow the person. Superior technique accounts for much of this redistribution of emphasis. Magnification, close-ups, long shots, tracking, and other camera movements make available to vision intimacies and vistas the theatergoer never sees. An ashtray full of cigarette stubs, a plane ticket in a coat pocket, clouds scudding across a glowering sky—all these things carry meaning on the screen but either could not be shown on the stage or would hardly be noticed without the actors tipping us off.

Theoretically, the movies can carry to an ultimate conclusion their replacement of living persons with lifeless images; they can focus so intensely on objects that they dispense altogether with human beings. A building on film can be as much a source of viewer fascination as the characters who inhabit it. The camera can dwell on its exterior and track through its empty rooms without sacrificing dramatic interest. A stage bare of men and women for any length of time would clear the house; but great films have been made without human actors, or with actors only as accessories.[70]

Is the cinema, then, an antihumanistic art, infatuated with matter, a medium of death and reification? And is this the explanation for its long love affair with the United States, the cutting edge of international capitalism?

## Death

There is no doubt that death haunts the cinema. The medium has a well-deserved reputation for violence and mayhem; no other art form can match it for body count. Blood-spattered heads and torsos, and piles of corpses, linger in the memory of every moviegoer. Fittingly, the spectator has to enter a blackened chamber to witness the scene of slaughter (or at least had to until the availability of the VCR). Lindsay shakes his head over this circumstance, struck in 1915 by the paradox of a young, energetic people "going for dreams into caves as shadowy as the tomb of Queen Thi."[71] (Poe, fantasist of premature interment, would have been delighted.)

The association of photographic reproduction with death precedes the movies: as Benjamin points out, early daguerreotypes were typically made in cemeteries because prolonged outdoors exposure with minimal distraction was necessary for the best results.[72] Today, the setting for watching a film is more funereal than those Parisian graveyards, and grimmer than anything Lindsay could have imagined. The screening rooms of mall multiplexes, many of them situated below ground level, are not unlike large coffins, cramped, box-shaped, and unadorned.[73]

Alternative interpretations of this morbidness suggest themselves. One reading, already touched on, would emphasize the cinema's filiations with the commodity, its collusion, as a technological art, with absence and the inorganic. Theorists of the commodity form from Marx to Lukács point out how, under capitalism, relations between persons are replaced by relations between things. Nonbeing supposedly reigns. The movies might be said to commodify both in their foregrounding of the object and in their power to persuade us that the figures on the screen are living human beings. We respond to the characters moving and conversing in front of us as though they were real people, when in actuality they are images imprinted on celluloid acetate. We invest them with human subjectivity, but they are merely simulacra, not even capable of returning our glance.

An objection to this analysis, other than noting the nostalgia for presence, might accuse it of confounding a hunger for immortality with a death instinct. The pictures flirt with extinction, our second interpretation holds, not because they are suffused with necrophilia, but on the contrary because they dream of banishing the fact of perishability. Part of their attraction consists in the very realism with which they represent death. (This was true of the American film industry from its origins, as in Edwin S. Porter's *The Great Train Robbery* [1903].) The screen's solemnity about killing, the straight face with which it refuses to allow its corpses to return for a bow at the performance's end, merely underlines its victory over mortality. The point is not that the fallen actor returns to life in a subsequent film. It is rather that the movies, particularly older ones, present us with the constant miracle of men and women who are literally dead rising and talking. The performers and their performances, unlike those on stage, last forever. They never lose their power to entertain.

The wish to defeat death is human, but what could be more American than the belief that you can really do it? American (or Californian) refusal to accept mortality has occasioned satire among European visitors, perhaps most memorably in three books by the English—Aldous Huxley's novel *After Many a Summer Dies the Swan* (1939), another novel, *The Loved One* (1948), by Evelyn Waugh, and Jessica Mitford's muckraking exposé of the funeral business, *The American Way of Death* (1963). The home of cinematic dreams has led the way in muzak piped into cemeteries and corpses stored at subfreezing temperatures, in the hope of scientific resurrection.

## Religion

Vanquishing death through the promise of eternal life is the desideratum of religious faith. The movies have been described as a substitute religion for twentieth-century urbanites, and some scholars have begun to treat the idea seriously, noting that movie houses, like churches, are public gathering places where moral values get negotiated. (My example of outwitting mortality on celluloid is open to more sympathetic interpretation, as a faith-fortifying experiment in the resurrection of the individual.) The cinematic image can also be seen as a latter-day variant of the religious painting, a man-made figuration that supplies a glimpse of an absent (and greater) reality.[74] Movies have an ontological compatibility with the spiritual or supernatural: they bring us into contact with bodiless presence. The art form that is the most sybaritic in its lifelike mimesis of the real is at the same time the most spectral and miraculous in its commerce with disembodiment.

No wonder Americans have taken so passionately to film! The world's leaders in materialism have no peers among postmodern peoples for piety. The United States consistently records the highest percentage of active church members of any industrialized nation. The British, a this-worldly people who take pride in their hard-headed empiricism, stand at the opposite end of the spectrum; in the 1950s, when the American figures were at their zenith, fewer than 10 percent of England's population regularly attended religious services.[75]

Alexis de Tocqueville believed that the two sides of American character, "religious insanity" and material acquisitiveness, were inextricably connected. It is predictable, he wrote, that a society bent upon possessing things should generate "an amazing reaction . . . in the souls of some men. . . . I should be surprised if mysticism did not soon make some advance among a people solely engaged in promoting their own worldly welfare."

A century and a half later, the movies put on display the paradoxical nature of a national community at once unreservedly earthbound and "fanatically spiritual."[76]

## Politics and Democracy

Another gloss on the effacement of the individual in the celluloid commodity can be derived from American political life. The "first new nation," as the United States has been called, carried the banner of modernity in its commitment to a politics of abstraction. The nation came into being as a rejection of allegiance to the British Crown, the colonists transferring the power once felt to inhere in special persons like King George the Third to the generality of the people as a whole, and embodying that power, not in individuals, but in elected offices and laws. Deference to personal prestige yielded to a political community in which truth was to be arrived at through reasoned judgment and debate.

Following Jürgen Habermas, we can understand this change as a "structural transformation of the public sphere." In America, the shift toward an impersonal polity was given additional impetus by the

Constitution, a document designed to address the problem of how to establish a republic in a large country, where direct participation by most citizens in governing was not feasible (nor desirable, according to the Founding Fathers). The revolutionary generation sought to curb the threat of immediacy by splitting up or diffusing authority. There were two aspects to this strategy. First, the Founders effected a division between the federal government and the states. They vested the most significant powers—to make war, to regulate commerce, and so on—in a distant, national government that was insulated from the people by the buffer of local or state politics. Second, they broke up the federal government itself into three independent branches, the executive, the legislature, and the judiciary. This tripartite structure further diluted the connection between the rulers and the ruled. No branch was sovereign, each could restrain the others, and the complex system of checks and balances that resulted made central authority invulnerable to the passions of popular will. It might appear at first that the British government is more protected from popular control than the American, more "remote" and centralized. Sovereignty is concentrated in Parliament (technically, the Queen, the Lords, and the Commons), and the electorate gets to cast its ballots for only one branch, the House of Commons. The prime minister, unlike the American president, is not elected by direct vote but instead chosen by the people's representatives in Parliament. Typically, those representatives neither live in nor stand for the interests of their constituencies, to which they are assigned by their party. They represent the party and vote according to its dictates, "not," as one political scientist has said in contrasting the English plan to the American one, "as independent or famous personalities or local spokesmen."77

Such qualifications duly noted, English political power is more accessible and "answerable" to the electorate—just as the stage player is more present and answerable to the theatergoing audience—*because* it is unitary. In actual practice, sovereignty resides in the Commons and its creations, the prime minister and the cabinet. The power that in the United States is dispersed twice over is fused in Britain: there is no regional government to speak of, and judges have no mandate of review over statutory law. The executive and the legislature cannot speak with discordant voices because they cannot be pried apart.

An English prime minister and cabinet are chosen by the party that has a majority in the Commons; they are dismissed the moment their majority vote evaporates. If the public dislikes what the government has done, it can turn out the ruling party (and with it the prime minister) in the next election and install a new one. Responsibility for behavior in office cannot be avoided. The American separation of powers minimizes direct redress of government as a whole. Walter Bagehot was exaggerating, but not by much, when he remarked many years ago, "The splitting of sovereignty into many parts amounts to there being no sovereign."[78] (Hypothetically, of course, political authority emanates from the people, which is to say that sovereignty is everywhere and nowhere.) The Congress—either the Senate or the House of Representatives, or both—can belong to a different party from the president. Justices sitting on the Supreme Court may have been appointed years earlier, by presidents from both parties. Where does responsibility for the government's record lie? How can the voter reach the source of political power?

The analogy between constitutional systems and forms of amusement is extensive. A residual but still potent attachment to persons persists in Britain, which has its peers and monarchy and its human players on the boards. The more direct link between public and performer, or voter and government, encourages a stronger feeling of participation in both areas. This is reflected in politics by the far greater percentage of eligible voters who exercise their right in Britain, some 75 percent in 1987 as compared to barely 50 percent in American presidential elections.[79] British politicians, like dramatic actors, are also more subordinate to their "roles" than their American counterparts. Party discipline is strict, so much so that the prime minister can be sacked by the party even without a parliamentary setback. And there is the larger function served by language in both the English government and the English theater. As Bagehot pointed out, because Parliament can remove the prime minister by defeating him on a major vote, Great Britain enjoys a higher degree of "Government by discussion" than does the United States. Debates occur in the American Congress, "but they are prologues without a play. There is nothing of a catastrophe about them; you cannot turn out the government."[80] (Impeachment, attempted only once and then unsuccessfully, would be the exception that proves the general rule of Congressional discursive fecklessness.)

On the American side, the remoteness and diffusion of the federal government, plus the fact that there is no ascriptive office, works to dissipate immediate personal influence; correspondingly, the culture excels at the deployment of animated images. Attenuation of the aura does not, however, liquidate charisma or curtail power. The American president is in no danger of being relieved by party and so is unconstrained by allegiance to it. (Contrast Clinton's indifference to Congressional Democrats to Thatcher's ouster by the Tories.) In his autonomy, he has more in common with the film star than with the stage actor.[81] But it is most of all the inaccessibility of the diegesis that unites the cinema with the multilayered American political order. The actors, filmic and political, perform in a cordoned-off domain largely impermeable to the spectators/electorate. A president or a congressman can be voted out, a film can be boycotted, but power to disrupt the unfolding narrative in either sphere is limited.

This is, perhaps, to overestimate the enclave-like nature of American democratic institutions. Emphasizing the shield around national government slights the leadership of the United States in political integration of the masses. Popular sovereignty triumphed, whatever barriers the Founders may have erected against it, and the new nation outpaced England, and most of Europe, in extending the suffrage to the people. Mobilization of mass sentiment became a necessity for political survival. The spectacle of electioneering, replete with parades, advertising, and mass parties, was already a fact of life by the second quarter of the nineteenth century (the Age of Jackson); comparable levels of popular participation were not attained in Britain until the passage of the Reform Acts of 1832, 1867, 1884, and 1918.

In Europe, where the ballot remained restricted for so long, culture was defined by the elite performative arts of the nineteenth or bourgeois century: concerts, opera, ballet, and the drama. (The vote was effectively if not legally limited in the United States too, on racial rather than economic grounds.) American democratic electoralism prepared the way for the less exclusive forms of entertainment that have proliferated in the twentieth century. One does not have to accept the more extravagant publicity for the cinema as a democratic art to agree that movies were cheap and inclusive enough to qualify as theater for the common people. "The American cinema," Pierre Renoir has said, "is essentially working class," but it would be more accurate to describe the post-nickelodeon motion pictures as classless. In the age of mass consumerism, this plebeian attraction has overspread the planet.[82]

## Being and Doing
### Meritocratic and Class Society

*Snobbery is the religion of England.*

—

FRANK HARRIS (1925)[83]

Fredric March, admonished for his stylized gestures while playing a scene for a film, is supposed to have responded, "I keep forgetting—this is a movie and I mustn't act."[84] March was joking, but he put his finger on an essential truth. The cinema is a medium of being, the drama an art of performance. Or rather, they are both arts of performance, but in cinema the self is performed, while the stage actor performs a role.

The reasons for this are partly technological. The close-up made possible by the camera permits a degree of intimate scrutiny that is unavailable in the theater. The stage actor seeking to communicate a particular emotion to an audience of several thousand doesn't enjoy the luxury of nuance. He or she must project vocally and gesture clearly in order to have a chance of being seen and heard. These ostentatious, mannered actions would appear unbelievable in a film. There the smallest expressive detail is visible everywhere in the auditorium: a raised eyebrow, a half-smile, a pursed lip. Thus the film actor, to seem natural, must keep acting to a minimum; in a sense he or she mustn't act at all but simply *be*. Or as Henry Fonda has said, "You do it just like in reality."[85]

In film, in other words, what matters is who you are; in the theater, what counts is what you do. (Tragedy, said Aristotle, in a celebrated definition applicable to all genres of the drama, is an "imitation of action.") Mastery of technique—trained voice, diction, movement, body control—is necessary for the stage but less important for the movies than appearance and personality. Stage actors can lose themselves in a character. Subordinating selfhood, they can pretend to be somebody else. The movie actor never quite metamorphoses into a different human being; the medium resists effacement, and some residual self always shines through. Stars like John Wayne and Clint Eastwood, who have flat voices and can command a relatively narrow range of emotions, would be disasters outside the silver screen. But in Hollywood westerns, they have few equals, and basically they play themselves in every picture.

The American cinema has cherished understatement in its performers almost from the beginning. As early as 1912, the approach to acting dictated by the close-up came to be known as the "American style" or "le plan americain." Restrained and psychological, it emerged as a deliberate contrast to the stage-influenced flamboyance of the primitive European cinema. Old-style French, Italian, and English actors got across meanings through stilted pantomime, a veritable encyclopedia of stock gestures and expressions that had been compiled over centuries. A contemporaneous commentator summarized the New World innovation:

> The difference between the two schools is broad and plain. The European school is based more upon bodily movements than upon the mobility of the face. The American school relies more upon the expression of the face and the suppression of bodily movement. It remained for the Americans to demonstrate that more dramatic emotion is the keynote of American pantomime.[86]

Forty years later, American experimentation with film's more understated acting requirements conferred an advantage in developing the style of performance known as "the Method" (originally a stage technique). Pioneered by a Russian, Konstantin Stanislavsky, Method acting was popularized during the 1950s by the Actors Studio in New York; its best-known practitioners are Marlon Brando, James Dean, and Paul Newman. The Method emphasizes emotional life over externals. In *On the Waterfront* (1954), Brando was challenged not to impersonate the dock worker Terry Malloy but rather to live him, so that his feelings would become indistinguishable from those of his character. Mumbled lines and awkward improvisations were taken as evidence of authenticity, conclusive demonstrations that the spectator was witnessing the emotional turmoil of a real person, the man named Marlon Brando.

Hence the American star system, a phenomenon not unique to the movies but one given a decisive assist by the cinema's foregrounding of the actor's personality. Everyone recognizes the name and face of Marlon Brando; few have any idea who "Terry Malloy" is. Genuine stars tower above their roles; regardless of whom they portray, they are always Brando, or Jim Carrey, or Katherine Hepburn. They impress us as being more alive, more real, than the most versatile performer on the stage.[87]

Significantly, the British cinema, which recruits its performers from the theater, has not been prolific at generating larger-than-life screen personalities. Laurence Olivier, Ralph Fiennes, and Emma Thompson qualify as English "stars," but none has the same mass appeal as the top American box office attractions. British film actors are apt to be just that, actors, appreciated more for their roles and histrionic range than for their looks and notoriety.

In two respects, then, film acting would seem to overturn the supposition of an America-movies/England-theater isomorphism. Movie stars, those compelling "presences" on the screen, take the cinematic form back in the direction of immediacy. They trouble the medium's presumed alliance with antinaturalist modernity. And second, an objection more pertinent for our concerns here, the film actor's "being" appears to clash with American folkways and to fit better with Englishness than the stage performer's "doing." In theory (if not always in fact), who you are—your family and breeding—counts less in the United States than what you do with yourself. America puffs itself as an achievement society, where the individual without pedigree can succeed through energy and initiative. (A short story by Hawthorne, "My Kinsman, Major Molineux" [1832], identifies this idea as the Republic's generative principle. A young man named Robin journeys to the city hoping to advance through the patronage of his uncle, the aristocratic-sounding Major Molineux. But after seeing his relative tarred and feathered in a revolutionary outbreak, the hero acknowledges his Americanism by remaining to seek his fortune on his own.)

In Britain, on the other hand, who you are matters a great deal to your chances in life. The English, who still maintain a monarchy and whose "lords" hold political office (considerably reduced in power, to be sure) by virtue of birth, place a high premium on inheritance and breeding. Accent, manners, and bearing make known a person's class background, and no amount of success in "doing" can open certain doors if he or she lacks the right bloodlines.

The first inconsistency, that the film star seems more present to the viewer than the stage actor does, can be easily disposed of. The illusion of cinematic immediacy is just that, an illusion, attributable to the persuasiveness of mechanical reproduction. Hollywood conventions are arguably *more* artificial than those operating in the theater; film acting's greater "realism" emerges in the cutting room. The standard means of representing movie dialogue, for example, is through the "shot-reverse-shot" pattern: one performer delivers his or her lines, face to the camera, and then the camera, reversing position, shows the second performer reacting. The second actor may not even be present when the first speaks, or vice versa. Both may have to address their words to an empty chair or a stand-in actor. While the "exchange" may be repeated a half-dozen times before the director feels satisfied, all the moviegoer gets to see is the finished scene constructed by the film editor: a seamless flow of utterance, response, and utterance. At least stage actors have to declaim their lines in sequence, as people do in real life.[88] It should be noted as well that the greater communicativeness of the film star's features, beheld in close-up, is itself a convention: people don't necessarily reveal their feelings in their faces. And, finally, what could be more American than the sacralizing and commodifying of personality in the star cult, the simultaneous transformation of human beings into religious idols and objects to be sold in the market?

As for the seemingly implausible notion of a parallel between film's accent on being and the American credo of self-reliance, simply to pose the question this way is to suggest that here, too, the inconsistency, or much of it anyway, dissolves upon inspection. In the United States the social order is understood to recognize and reward merit; achievement (or doing) is a *function* of who you are. Intrinsic selfhood, analogous to the personality of the screen star, encompasses intelligence, talent, character, and capacity for hard work. It is these intangible things—not family, nor genealogy, nor education, nor even connections—that are supposed to determine how far you can go in life. Performance flows, as it were, from being; you succeed or fail because you deserve to.

Robin's error, in the Hawthorne story cited earlier, is to imagine that someone who is not himself, a family member, Major Molineux, can win him a place in the world. But this belief is a legacy of the English past, and Independence swept away such relics. Robin will have to prosper "without the help of [his] kinsman, Major Molineux." Hawthorne gives his youthful protagonist no surname because he believes that in the new nation family or patronym is irrelevant. Merit, and merit alone, is what shepherds the American on his quest through life.

In short, it might be argued that far from clashing with American values, the movie star's apparent self-identity is an ideological corollary, an apotheosizing in the zone of popular entertainment of the dogma of individualism. More, one could contend—somewhat hyperbolically— that the cinematic privileging of being is an exercise in mystification. Movie acting lends confirmation to the questionable idea that the individual's inherent capacity determines his or her lot. But talent and recompense are seldom so neatly matched. The star's personality, after all, is a creation of technology, editorial cutting and splicing, and marketing; the sense that we know who our heroes *really* are expresses more fantasy than truth. To pursue the analogy, how many "self-made" men in American industry owe their fortunes less to innate merit than to parental advantages, connections, and luck? How often is entrepreneurial genius as much an ex-post-facto fabrication as is integrity or courage on the screen?

Correspondingly, the premeditation of Brando's "authentic" performance in *On the Waterfront* points up the artifice of even the most natural screen personae. While some kind of instinctive Method has always been operative in the movies, it is far from certain that Brando's most admired aleatory moments were impromptu. The famous scene where he slips his hand into Edie Doyle's (Eva Marie Saint's) glove, for example, telegraphing his character's muffled sensitivity (and sexuality), probably has more to do with the direction of Elia Kazan than it does with the Academy Award–winning actor's inner being.[89]

On the other side, the theater's commitment to impersonation links up with the class character of English society. To Hawthorne, as we have seen, the principle of patronage was a colonial residue, suited to the mother country but not to America. Attitudes are different today, but they are not so altered that Margaret Thatcher couldn't launch her "conservative" revolution against the perdurability of the patronage ethos, endeavoring to wean her countrymen from tradition and turn them into American-style entrepreneurs. The case of Thatcher, ostensibly a foe of English "being," is especially revealing. Even in her urgency to modernize, the former prime minister's choices in personnel suggest how difficult it has been to dislodge the English from their attachment to an ascriptive social order.

No American politician would dare bring before the electorate a set of advisers with the elitist credentials of those assembled by Thatcher. Arthur Marwick, in his history of postwar British society, notes "the overwhelmingly upper-class composition" of her first cabinet. With few exceptions, the members had been educated at Oxford or Cambridge and at exclusive "public" schools like Harrow, Winchester, and Charterhouse. Many had peerages in their families; most owned country estates and held directorships. Richard Nixon and Ronald Reagan, who effected a similar antiestablishment shake-up in the American Republican Party, culled advisers from the Eastern elite but also had their Agnews and Haldemans, their Meeses and Deavers.[90]

The English fealty to class, a disposition by no means confined to the upper echelons, holds the key to a mode of doing more in line with the theater's virtuosity than the screen's self-reference. Class in Great Britain is, among other things, a matter of performance. It involves accommodating oneself to a style, learning the varieties of behavior appropriate to one's social position. Marwick quotes liberally from people belonging to the whole spectrum of class identities, all of whom (in the 1960s and 1970s) were sensitive to the subtle lines demarcating them from class outsiders: the habits of socializing, the kinds of food, the preferences in sports and recreation, the use of language, the choice of books to read, etc.[91] In the fifties, the unerring classification of persons by both identifiable and virtually invisible traits became a cause for satire, as in Nancy Mitford's famous collection *Noblesse Oblige*, where the English were grouped as "U" or "non-U" (upper class or not) according to differences of speech. ("Radio" and "sweet" indicated non-U, "wireless" and "pudding" a member of the aristocracy.) A self-ironizing jest, to be sure, but one with a serious undercurrent; as Evelyn Waugh explained in his contribution to the Mitford book, "In England class distinctions have always roused higher feelings than national honour; they have always been the subject of feverish but very private debate."[92]

The English social perspective might be summed up in the idea that "doing" is a species of iteration or *inauthenticity*, of mastering a role that has been scripted from outside the self. It is not a manifestation of personality or "being" on the American model. Doing for the English doesn't issue from one's inherent capacities but rather constitutes the self as the enactment of an already existing scenario; it is closely homologous with the classical acting style of the stage performer. One learns a part, and the part becomes who one is. To revise our previous formulation, the English self is a function of prescriptive doing; in the United States, the self is the ground of performance.

Admittedly, exceptions abound. The borders between English classes are certainly more fluid than they were in the nineteenth century, probably more so than in the 1970s. And the English, like Americans, pride themselves on rewarding ability; one historian sees them as evolving into a society of professionals.[93] Thatcher was a philo-Semite who respected Jews for their work ethic, and her subsequent cabinets had a more socially diverse makeup than her first one. But class distinctions have proven unusually resilient in Britain, where descendants of the great banking, commercial, and industrial familes of the past continue to staff the elite. The divisions have produced a culture where playing the role as well as one can has often been more admired than independent exertion. Marwick, again, is an indispensable guide to the English predilection for class theatricality: "formality and authority in other industrialized societies are related to function: a boss behaves like a boss because he is a boss. In Britain a boss behaves as he does because he belongs to, or has been socialized into, a particular social background."[94]

The English/American dualism can be correlated with the historical change from character to personality. At the end of the last century, a traditional idea of character—understood as honor, work, deeds, and duty—gave ground to a new method of self-presentation. The reconceived individual strove to be more expressive and self-conscious; he or she took pride in the cultivation of qualities such as poise, charm, sincerity, and magnetism. Though hardly limited to the United States, the emergent ethos spread quickly there and found a home in the movies. While the English and their theater preserved elements of the older character type, the American cinema furthered the fascination with the performing self's uniqueness that became endemic to the "culture of personality." Early film stars were highy sensitive to the altered requirements for desirability. Douglas Fairbanks Sr. had the secret of celebrity down pat: he "was dedicated not to his art but to himself." The movies helped to terminate what had been a given of Western society for millennia: the connection between fame and achievement.[95]

The great English actor Sir Laurence Olivier has best articulated the contrast between dramaturgical (and national) styles. In 1967, in an interview for the BBC, Olivier described himself as a performer who works from "the outside in." The peripheral technique he shares with kindred spirits like Alec Guinness can be distinguished, said Olivier, from the approach of most movie stars, who usually "start from the inside." The stage actor accumulates a host of external details until a character emerges; the film actor has to be "interior" and reserved because of the "microscopic" interrogation of the camera. Whereas a practitioner of the Method, an American like Brando, is "more likely to find himself in the parts he plays," the external actor prefers "to find the parts in himself; perhaps not necessarily in himself, but simply to find the parts, go out to them and get them, and *be* somebody else."[96]

To conclude with a pardonable exaggeration: Americans are a people of Brandos, always playing themselves, wherever their selves may lead them; the English are a nation of Oliviers, adapting to and submerging themselves in the parts that define their identities.

## Afterthought on Being and Doing

It might be objected to the above argument that the movie actor is far more of a "doer," as the word is commonly used, than any stage player. What is it that a film star *cannot* do? Return from the dead (*Diabolique*, 1955), ride a bicycle across the sky (*E.T.: The Extra Terrestrial*, 1982), battle aliens and come away victorious (*Independence Day*, 1996), give birth to the Antichrist (*Rosemary's Baby*, 1968), be romanced by a fifty-foot-tall ape (*King Kong*, 1933)—all have been done on celluloid (and may be outdone in the future) and all with a degree of verisimilitude that no drama can duplicate. But of course all these wondrous goings-on are at the same time more factitious than an exchange of dialogue on the stage. They are not the actions of the performers but the contrivances of stunt men, trick shots, doubles, camera angles, and special effects. No one believes that Tom Cruise can really pilot a jet fighter; no one who has seen her on Broadway in *Victor, Victoria* doubts that Julie Andrews can carry a tune. Andrews is prized for her singing ability, along with her other skills; Cruise is a star because he plays Tom Cruise.[97]

## The Movies and the Novel (Part I)

Some readers will have noticed that many of the statements made here about the cinema as an art of displacement apply to the novel as well. Indeed, it might be postulated that the novel is to verbal storytelling, and to oral culture generally, as film is to the theater. The similarities are historical as well as structural. That is, not only does the novel resemble the movies constitutively, in its substitution of mediation for presence, it foreshadows them, at least in the American experience, in the way it emerged and evolved as an aesthetic form. The histories of the two arts exhibit certain shared features that may be common to all or most ascendant cultural technologies (in these particular instances, the mechanical reproduction of linguistic narrative and of moving images).

This is not to claim that the theater is a moribund institution, destined to be extinguished by the cinema much as oral storytelling melted away before the book. Or rather, if recognition of the stage's premodernity has been fundamental to this essay, there is no corresponding implication that the drama will disappear, its functions usurped in their entirety by the silver screen. Premodern arts and activities remain an integral feature of modern lives. Moreover, a better argument can be made that the proper sequence is not so much stage to film as prose fiction to film, with the movies as the twentieth-century successor to the nineteenth-century novel as the foremost cultural grammar of its time. While the theater *approximated* fiction's nonpresence at the height of Great Britain's empire, in the longer view it was the novel that accompanied and embroidered the English people's rise to global power. Dickens and Austen were the voices of English hegemony, just as Capra and Coppola have been the cinematic celebrants of the American century.

Both media, novel and cinema, fastened on representational accuracy as their defining quality. The novel purported to be scientific and up-to-date because, unlike the medieval romance, it was based on fact and dedicated to verisimilitude. Novels eschewed miracles, dragons, and impossibly virtuous or wicked characters. They related the real adventures of real human beings. *The History of So-and-So* was a formulaic title, "A Tale of Truth" a standard subtitle.

As it underwent Americanization, the new genre met with controversy and resistance. (It had to weather opposition in Britain, too.) Imported originally from the mother country—Richardson's *Pamela* (1740–41), in an edition overseen by the leading colonial printer, Benjamin Franklin, was the first book of prose fiction published in America—the novel quickly came to be viewed as morally problematic, addicted to sensational and salacious narratives that lured the unthinking into imitative misconduct. Novels were consumed in solitude, away from the supervision of authorities, and they appealed to, or, in the opinion of critics, pandered to, the most impressionable members of society—women and the young. Further, they conspired with other unwholesome developments, such as a craving for luxuries, to corrode feelings of public responsibility. Novels bred habits of passivity because they were essentially nonrecriprocal: readers were powerless to affect what happened on the page. In short, clergymen, educators, and statesmen agreed that the appetite for printed stories augured a reign of privatism and self-indulgence that could destroy the republic.

At the same time, primitive American novels retained many of the customary qualities of verbal culture. Fiction's shady reputation discouraged authorial acknowledgment, and so the books were often anonymous and ephemeral, issued without identifying copyright and printed in amateurish and hastily assembled editions that have disappeared without a trace. Oral literature's stress on utility remained strong in the new genre, anxious as it was to rebut the charge of worthlessness. Early fiction loudly boasted of its pedagogic benefits, and moral exhortation and the purveying of information were its earmarks. Consumption, if typically private, was not exclusively so. A cautionary tale by Hannah Foster might be read aloud to family members or to a group of friends, and early readers still had enough of a sense of participation to fill the margins of their favorite texts with scribbled responses. But many readers did not own the books, which were priced too high for popular purchase; instead they rented works of fiction for a small fee from social or circulating libraries.

On balance, what this history suggests is that the novel's primary or perhaps "manifest" emphasis (to plagiarize a psychological category) proclaims its modernity. The form treasures realism; it counts on popular acceptance, attracting audiences that were historically excluded from elite culture; it deals not in presence but in technological impersonality; and it accelerates the commodifying of art. But the novel also has a secondary or "latent" dimension, redolent of the verbal formation that preceded it. This side of the genre involves it in sociabilty, moral didacticism, and nonownership. And although these latent aspects may be more traditional, even old-fashioned, they continue to characterize certain kinds of novels and sizable groups of readers.

So, too, the movies include dominant and recessive components that might be labeled modern and traditional; so, too, they have a history of disreputable association and elite hostility. Early filmmakers bowed to empirical accuracy as piously as did Daniel Defoe or Susanna Rowson. Shooting "on location" was a convention from the first, much emphasized in advertisements for the medium's truthfulness. Technical advisers, carefully reproduced costumes, and "original participants" like William S. Hart, the first silent-western star (who was in fact not a cowboy but a professional actor), bolstered the claim of authenticity. President Woodrow Wilson exemplified the public's awestruck response to cinematic realism. After a White House screening of *The Birth of a Nation*, he is supposed to have declared, "It is like writing history with Lightning."[98]

Yet as with the novel, the earliest movies aroused a storm of condemnation. (The detractors continue to this day.) Observers deplored the clientele, the setting, and the subject matter. The nickelodeons, at five or ten cents a show, were priced well below live entertainment. They had a huge following among the immigrant working classes (who didn't need to know English to appreciate silent pictures), and women comprised a high proportion of the viewers. These unsupervised souls should have been outdoors enjoying the fresh air. Instead they congregated in unsanitary, sexually mixed arenas where the darkness concealed illicit behavior. They stared at violent, erotic images. The cinema, complained the social worker Jane Addams, was a "house of dreams" that stimulated unattainable desires and disqualified young people for the real world.[99]

However glamorized the images, the early movie theaters themselves were not zones of the unapproachable. As noted previously, the new technology, like the printed story, eliminated the flesh-and-blood performer more in theory than in actual practice; the drift toward atomistic disembodiment was contested by a residual ethos of participation. In the nickelodeons, lectures or group activities like patriotic songs formed a regular part of the evening's fare. Live vaudeville acts might alternate with short films, and spectators, especially in the days before sound, would talk loudly among themselves. Stamping, hissing, and cheering made known the public's reactions. Vachel Lindsay considered the interactive spirit so important to moviegoing that he proposed "taking a nightly ballot on the favorite film or episode."[100]

Nor did the ethos of individualism have an open field on the screen itself. No credits accompanied very early pictures, and the identities of actors and directors were unknown. This policy seems to have had the endorsement of the performers. Must had backgrounds in the stage and feared that association with film's lowly status would damage their theatrical careers. They allowed themselves to appear in the new art form only on condition of anonymity.[101]

The communality of the cinematic experience dissipated over time. Just as the novel shed such residues of oral storytelling as didacticism and direct address to the reader, so the pictures moved away from their dependence on participatory elements. Sound emanating from the screen imposed quiet on the audience; live entertainment was banished; the visual scene of action became a sealed-off world; and the star system assigned names to faces.

This historical pattern has been more or less repeated throughout the cinema's existence. Working-class and immigrant theaters—at the turn of the century, during the 1920s, and again at the present time (the 1990s)—have perpetuated elements of intimacy seemingly at odds with mechanical reproduction, only to see those elements evicted by modernization. The nickelodeon's exuberance subsided into middle-class sobriety and the Hollywood style. The neighborhood movie houses of ethnic Chicago, with their amateur nights and Italian or Polish sing-alongs, were displaced, in the New Deal period, by intimidating palaces staffed by ushers in formal attire.[102] And in today's immigrant Chinese and Indian communities, say those in Boston or New York, talking, eating, and general audience commotion deflect attention from the screen. Presumably as their devotees Americanize and disperse to the suburbs, these convivial settings will go the route of their predecessors.

And yet the advent of the VCR might suggest otherwise. With home viewing challenging the night out at the movies, the interactive ambience, which we have denominated as residual or traditional, has reemerged as perhaps inherently *more* in step with the technological imperative than the impersonal cineplex. As they watch rented films on TV sets in their own dwellings, families and friends converse, blurt out their reactions, snack or eat meals, come and go. They re-create the nickelodeon's "pre-talkie" gregariousness.[103] Another way of putting this would be to say that the latent, participatory dimension of moviegoing has overtaken its manifest, abstracted side. It would be as though novels had migrated back toward their oral roots and were still read aloud to groups of listeners. (In fact, this is precisely how many people now have the experience of "reading" fiction. They listen to novels on tape in their cars or while they prepare dinner at home. Storytelling has been resurrected by technology.)

The cinema in its vernal phase replicated not only the early novel's clubbishness but also its extreme vulnerability. In effect, primitive pictures had not fully separated from the impermanence of live performance. Mechanisms of preservation were rudimentary, and controversy impeded the codifying of legal protection. At least as many late nineteenth and early twentieth-century films have been lost to posterity as preromantic fictions; barely one fifth of the total output from this era still exists. Griffith's current stature is owing partly to the happy survival rate of his works. He released roughly 495 titles, of which we have 485; more typical is the plight of Allan Dwan, who directed 120 pictures for the American Film Company in 1912 and is represented today by just *two* from that year. Struggles over ownership, both of the technology and of individual films, contributed to the high incidence of mortality. Thomas Edison's attempt to claim a monopoly through the Motion Picture Patents Company was defeated by the courts in 1915. And the first copyright law for moving pictures wasn't passed until 1912.[104]

In the area of durability, the VCR marks an apparent break with early film and a startling convergence with the novel. (As we shall see in the section on "Memory and Culture," the rupture is more chimerical than actual.) The new machine permits an experience, moviegoing, to revamp itself as a vendible ware, the videocassette, that one can own and touch. Or to be more precise, it converts a pure experience into a combined commodity *and* experience—thus imparting to the movies the ontological dualism of the book. The videocassette even approximates the novel in size and appearance. It comes with a caselike cover and can be stored in a library or on a bookshelf. Ironically, this cutting-edge technology reverts to the condition of the first American fictions in its imperfect status as mass consumer good. The majority of early novels were rented rather than purchased; videotapes, though their prices continue to drop, remain too costly for most people to buy on a regular basis. Rentals outnumber sales by a ratio of about nine to one.[105]

The videotape further imitates prose fiction in the site of its consumption: the private residence. Films have devolved from theater-like public showings with the nickelodeon to novel-like seclusion with the VCR. They draw near to the printed narrative's defining novelty: they enable consumption *in the home* of representations of the world *outside the home*. The movies, in addition to being a kind of shop window, provide a window on external reality. Before the VCR the spectator had to leave his or her domicile to enjoy this visual entrée into unknown vistas and experiences. Videotapes resituate the origin of the moviegoer's outward gaze in the domestic sphere; and in doing so, they recapitulate a basic self-reflexive trope of nineteenth-century fiction, what Raymond Williams refers to as "mobile privatization," the capacity to travel effortlessly into the larger world while remaining safely ensconced in interior space.[106]

How many Victorian-era stories begin with a character sitting in a room and peering through a window into the city or garden or house next door, expressing through that gesture the act of novel-reading itself? Two examples from the American tradition can stand for many on both sides of the Atlantic: the narrator of Poe's "Man of the Crowd," staring into the bustling London street outside his snug coffee house (and then rushing into the thoroughfare to join the mass); and Ellen Montgomery, heroine of Susan Warner's *The Wide, Wide World* (1850), looking wistfully from the window of her home at the vast and forbidding social world into which her mother's fatal illness will shortly plunge her.

A reasonable conclusion might be, then, that late twentieth-century film has gravitated structurally toward the Victorian novel because the two arts are animated by a kindred spirit. The spirit is that of imperialist suzerainty, of secondhand dominion from the metropole (a theme to be developed later). English readers were, and American spectators are, potentates of the visible universe. They need never leave their dwellings to command the world, on the page or on videotape, and observe it stretch out submissively before them. The Victorian novel, we should remember, flamed forth in many countries, but no where did it burn so brightly as in three of the great European empires of the previous century—France, England, and Russia. (The other major empire, the

Hapsburg, was less prolific of prose fiction.) And no nation, in this century overawed by the American eagle, has approached the filmmaking
prowess of the United States.

## The Movies and the Novel (Part II)

This century has produced a plethora of Hollywood novels as well as
innumerable fictions about film stars, moviemaking, and moviegoing.
The sympathy between prose narrative and the movies stands in contrast to the relative paucity of serious modern novels about theatrical
experience, Broadway or the London stage in particular. Fiction writers
were once intrigued by the thematic possibilities of the drama, which
they often saw as an analogue to their own project of storytelling. Some
of the greatest English-language novelists of the past, from Samuel
Richardson through Charles Dickens to Theodore Dreiser, experi-
mented with theater-related devices, tropes, and settings. But the present-day novel, attentive as always to the fabric of contemporaneous life,
has transferred its affections to the screen. Theater novels *have* been
written in the age of cinema, but most fall into the thriving *sub*-subgenre
of Broadway mysteries. Among serious or major writers, the subject has
gone the way of fox hunting and the clipper ship. The chief exceptions
are British.

As for the Hollywood or movie novel, it will come as no surprise that
the subgenre has bloomed most luxuriantly in the United States. The
first such work, a children's tale by the pseudonymous Victor Appleton,
*Tom Swift and His Wizard Camera*, appeared in 1912.[107] The list of those
who followed includes some of the biggest names in the modern
American canon: John Dos Passos (*The Big Money*, 1938), Nathanael
West (*The Day of the Locust*, 1939), F. Scott Fitzgerald (*The Last Tycoon*,
1941), Norman Mailer (*The Deer Park*, 1955), Gore Vidal (*Myra
Breckinridge*, 1968; *Myron*, 1974; *Hollywood*, 1990), and John Updike (*In
the Beauty of the Lilies*, 1996). Budd Schulberg was not of this caliber, but
he has two superior books to his credit: *What Makes Sammy Run* (1941)
and *The Disenchanted* (1950). Vladimir Nabokov's *Laughter in the Dark*

(1938) concerns a cinema usherette who hopes for a film career. (The novel had been published in Russia seven years earlier as *Camera Obscura*.) The poet Stephen Vincent Benét took a stab at Hollywood fiction (*The Beginning of Wisdom*, 1921). Walker Percy won a National Book Award for *The Moviegoer* (1961), his story about a New Orleans stockbroker who is addicted to the movies. Other noteworthy American novelists who have tackled the subject are William Boyd, Charles Bukowski, Jay Cantor, R. V. Cassill, Robert Coover, Joan Didion, John Gregory Dunne, Leslie Epstein, Oscar Hijuelos, Wright Morris, Craig Nova, William Saroyan, and Terry Southern.

Britons who have taken a fling at fictionalizing the sun-drenched "city of dreams" have tended to be expatriates. Aldous Huxley (whose *After Many a Summer Dies the Swan* has already been mentioned) settled in California, and both P. G. Wodehouse (author of *Laughing Gas*, 1938) and Christopher Isherwood (who wrote *Prater Violet* [1945], a novella that is one of the best examples of the form) became American citizens. Martin Amis, a British novelist who has *not* expatriated, describes a failed attempt to produce a feature film in *Money* (1985).

Fiction about the drama, on the other hand, has positively flooded from English pens. The connection goes back to the novel's beginnings: Richardson has his heroine attend the theater in the second part of *Pamela* (1740–41). (She shows her moral fiber by disapproving of the spectacle.) The protagonist of Fanny Burney's *Evelina* (1778) also pays a visit to the London stage. Jane Austen's characters regularly "play at theatricals," as the genteel pastime of acting in amateur productions was known in the nineteenth century (see *Mansfield Park* [1814] and *Emma* [1816]). Dickens, who had a passion for the stage and liked to manage and act in amateur entertainments himself, used theater scenes in many of his novels, including *Nicholas Nickleby* (1839) and *Great Expectations* (1861). (In a scandal that horrified his Victorian readers, Dickens left his wife for a young actress, Ellen Ternan, whom he had met at a fund-raising theatrical.) The heroine of Charlotte Brontë's *Villette* (1853), Lucy Snowe, is a governess who performs as a cross-dressing actress. *Daniel Deronda* (1876) teems with singers and stage players and likens the history of the Jews to a piece of theater, a "National Tragedy." (Eliot's "husband," George Henry Lewes, was the most influential English drama critic of his time.) One could mention as well Wilkie Collins, Oscar Wilde, and Ford Madox Ford.[108]

Nineteenth- and early twentieth-century American novelists also gravitated to the stage, with some of the most distinguished dabbling at playwriting. The saga of Henry James's disappointments as a dramatist has often been told; he essayed both original works and adaptations of his novels. Quite as prolific as a writer for the theater was James's fellow realist, William Dean Howells, who anticipated Shaw with his one-act discussion plays.[109] Both men also dealt with the stage in their fiction, as did—among many others—Stephen Crane (Maggie's trip to the popular melodrama with her suitor Pete), Edith Wharton (whose Lily Bart, the protagonist of *The House of Mirth* [1905], performs in tableaux), and Theodore Dreiser (Carrie Meeber, the heroine of *Sister Carrie* [1900], achieves stardom as an actress). Twain's two great charlatans in *Adventures of Huckleberry Finn* (1884), the King and the Duke, mangle Shakespeare and put on a comic production of "The Royal Nonesuch." And Melville's Ahab, whose rhetoric more grandly echoes Shakespeare, enters to stage directions and delivers soliloquies.

But fictional output on the theater, especially by Americans, has dropped off sharply in the twentieth century. There are collections of Broadway stories by Damon Runyon and Garson Kanin, and a Booth Tarkington novel called *Presenting Lily Mars* (1932). Leslie Epstein's *Regina* (1982) concerns a stage actress. After that one descends fairly rapidly to detective stories by the likes of New York's former mayor Ed Koch, author of *Murder on Broadway* (1995). The English are better represented. The most eminent name is Virginia Woolf, whose last work, *Between the Acts* (1941), has as its centerpiece the annual village pageant at Pointz Hall. A. S. Byatt's *The Virgin in the Garden* (1978) interweaves the Elizabethan drama with contemporary comedy, and Claire Rayner has written a multivolume family chronicle, "The Performers." Penelope Fitzgerald, highly regarded in Britain and with a growing reputation here, is the author of a delightful comic novel, *At Freddie's* (1982), about London's Temple Stage School, supplier of child actors for the West End. The vaudeville star, Dan Leno, appears as a character in Peter Ackroyd's thriller, *Dan Leno and the Limehouse Golem* (1994).

Brief glances at two books, one by Updike, one by Penelope Fitzgerald, will illustrate how the novel rings the changes on the United States-cinema/United Kingdom-theater contrast. *In the Beauty of the Lilies* tells a thoroughly American story about this country's century-long infatuation with the movies. For Updike, the movies *are* America, or have become a substitute religion for Americans. When the Rev. Clarence Wilmot, the first of the four Wilmot generations covered in the narrative, resigns from the ministry, he begins killing time in a local movie theater, "a church," as it strikes him, "with its mysteries looming brilliantly, undeniably above the expectant rows."[110] The man who lost his faith reading skeptical tomes in a book-lined study ends up staring at moving images projected on a white screen. His fate predicts America's devolution into a media-addicted society where literacy is a visual rather than a verbal skill.

In a nice touch, Clarence's unambitious son, Teddy, takes a job delivering mail—stranded in a backwater, as it were, of written communication. Teddy feels little of his father's entrancement before the screen. Film frightens him with its hyperbolic images of pleasure and destruction. But Teddy's daughter Essie is eager to reclaim the intensified world that her grandfather found so beguiling. She becomes the Hollywood star Alma DeMott, for whom the movies are a keener and more glorious reality than reality itself.

The last of the Wilmots is the dropout Clark, who grows up while another movie star, Ronald Reagan, occupies the White House. Clark returns to a parody of his great grandfather's abandoned faith by joining a Waco-like fundamentalist Temple where he ultimately perishes. To Clark, the distinction between film and nonfilm has lost all meaning. He believes that "reality is a kind of movie the self projects," and the final thought that occurs to him before he is killed is a quotation from Humphrey Bogart's character in *Casablanca*.[111] Clark's apocalyptic death recalls the cataclysmic last pages of West's *The Day of the Locust*; it is the kind of violent ending we expect from the motion pictures.

The title of Fitzgerald's novel refers to Frieda (or Freddie) Wentworth, the owner-manager of the acting school for children. Here, too, a cultural idiom is identified with nationhood. A painted canvas with lines from Shakespeare's *King John*, "Naught shall make us rue if England to itself do rest but true," hangs on a wall at Freddie's. Fidelity to England means honoring its dramatic tradition. "Without a great theatre you never have a great nation,"[112] as Freddie likes to say, and she herself is a masterful offstage actress who embodies the novel's commitment to performance, to brilliant impersonation rather than humorless sincerity. The point is underscored in the romance subplot. The stubbornly authentic teacher Pierce Carroll courts but loses his attractive fellow teacher Hannah Graves; the easygoing, fibbing character actor Boney Lewis wins her love.

Freddie's most talented student, Jonathan, works at his roles (like Olivier, whom he—or Fitzgerald—has clearly read) "from the outside inwards." Jonathan has no interest in Method self-absorption. To him,

> the surface is not superficial. He didn't want to know what it felt like to be desperate enough to jump from a wall; he wanted to know what someone looked like when they did it. From a walk, from a hesitation, from a nervous gesture, from breathing and silence, actors of Jonathan's sort understand the human predicament.

Jonathan's rival at the school is a brash and narcissistic young man named Mattie; he can fix his mind on nothing *but* himself. Jonathan, we are told, goes on to an estimable career on the London stage. Mattie becomes "a celebrity in every country where conditions were sufficiently settled for movies to be shown."[113]

*At Freddie's* treasures the ephemerality and community of the theater, suggesting that the two qualities are inextricably related. When a performance comes to life, Fitzgerald says, it establishes a momentary contact between the actors and the audience, a spell that lasts for an hour or two and is then "lost for eternity. The extravagance of that loss was its charm." But it seems that the charm of the transient has a limited appeal for the modern age. That, at any rate, is the conclusion Freddie herself arrives at. She informs her would-be financial backer, the hardbitten businessman Joey Blatt, that the Temple School will no longer teach Shakespeare. Henceforth she will only train children for TV commercials. As the aghast Blatt sputters in protest, Freddie explains that her eyes have been opened "to the future." The future belongs to the mass media. "There mustn't be a future without Freddie's."[114]

## Memory and Culture

Stanley Cavell begins his foreword to the enlarged edition of *The World Viewed* by remarking that he wrote the book "out of the memory of films"; hence his descriptions of particular sequences, in those days before the VCR, are "liable to contain errors." Far from apologizing for this situation, Cavell takes pride in it. He speculates that the inaccuracies in his account are themselves revealing about the movies under study, or about his experience of those movies. Such lapses may indicate something about film's "unpredictability." Cavell adds that "not about novels or stories or poems or plays, would we accept so casual and sometimes hilariously remote an account as we will about movies."[115] Cavell's emphasis on memory, or rather defense of forgetfulness, would seem to capture an important truth about the movies—a truth that may further clarify the differences between America's film-centered society and Britain's "empire of the stage." Attributing his flawed recollections to film's "orality," Cavell makes much of the gulf between the movies and those other arts—novels, poetry, plays—that are widely available in printed form. And we might want to agree that moviegoing begets a postmodern verbal culture. People take enormous pleasure in talking about films with each other (conversation about the medium may be the secular equivalent of seventeenth-century Puritans dissecting their minister's sermons), and seldom do they have in hand the printed texts of the titles being discussed. Until fairly recently, film scripts were the least accessible aesthetic genre. Most didn't survive even in manuscript, and precious few found their way into print. It was not uncommon to encounter a film buff who had never read one.

Consider the contrasting fate of the drama. Ostensibly the most verbal of the arts (along with opera), plays have their first life in writing, as scripts, and great numbers make the transition into books. The major living playwrights in England and America—Miller, Shepard, Pinter,

Stoppard, David Hare—can all be purchased in paperbound editions. And the greatest playwright of them all, Shakespeare, has generated a veritable print industry: paperbacks, scholarly editions festooned with notes, appendices, variant readings, etc., complete works, concordances, textual controversies, and more criticism and scholarship than anyone could plow through in a lifetime. Accuracy and knowledge of detail are the adjuncts of an artistic regime in which evanescent oral performances are preserved in printed books.

One might attempt to correlate these contrasting styles with the two societies where they prevail. Paucity of historical memory, or even an inability to remember what came before at all, is often taken to be a characteristic American failing. Americans have a reputation (whether deserved or not) for being indifferent to their country's past and ignorant about events that occurred before their lifetimes. (Who has not read of those high school seniors who report on questionnaires that the Civil War was fought in the twentieth century?) Whereas English guidebooks tout bygone times as a vital part of the national heritage, the hypothetical average American is oriented toward the present and future. The United States, having defined itself as escape from the past, has an ideological stake in wiping the slate clean. Ours is the land of the "fresh start," of sloughing off the burden of history and beginning anew.

But even if we grant that cultural forgetfulness is distinctively American, we should look more closely at Cavell's assumptions about film and the treachery of remembrance. In focusing on the movies' orality, Cavell has singled out as constitutive a temporary and, it may be, unrepresentative phase of both the genre and its consumption. It can be argued that the VCR—and my analysis of film and the novel intimates as much—represents, not a quirk of cinematic development, but a logical and necessary growth of the medium. To put it another way, the videocassette is both a present-day analogue to the nineteenth-century novel as imperial artifact *and* an elaboration of the cinema's dominant nature as the cultural form of modernity. It would follow that overcoming forgetfulness through mechanical means, an accomplishment of the VCR, expresses the American propensity. Historical amnesia leaves Americans unconcerned not because theirs is a culture of ephemera, but on the contrary because memorizing has so little role to play in modern existence.

Many commentators have noticed, for example, that the movies have always had a tendency toward commodification and discrete identity. These qualities were visible well before the invention of VCR technology. The transience of early films, like that of early novels, stemmed more from the callow state of the art, its incomplete differentiation from earlier modalities (theater, vaudeville, lantern shows, dioramas, etc.), than from any inherent insubstantiality. This might seem a counterfactual statement about a form of entertainment that moves and, until videotapes, couldn't be touched: how can an experience of shifting images *not* be fleeting? But a moment's reflection reminds us that the movies, unlike plays, are composed of shots rather than scenes. With proper equipment, the individual frames can be frozen for study, excision, and rearrangement. It is true that the ordinary viewer couldn't command this expensive technology (although many people did own home screens and projectors during the forties and fifties). Yet films could still be seen more than once, on TV or in second-run theaters, and seen in the identical form of their original viewing. Such iterability has never been possible with plays, which in their realization as performances are always unique: to see a revival or later production of *Death of a Salesman* (1949) is to see a *different* incarnation of that work.

Moreover, the earlier claim about the unavailability of movie scripts has to be revised in light of the cataract of such texts to descend upon bookstores in the 1980s and 1990s (or roughly since the diffusion of the VCR). Paperbound editions of scripts, often embellished with photographs, are now timed for publication with the opening of films, as an integral part of the promotion and commodifying of visual experience. Gore Vidal's statement, "Today, where literature was movies are," is only half true: movies have themselves become a branch of literature and, in chains like Barnes and Noble, are steadily encroaching upon the shelf space once reserved for novels and dramas.[116]

For all its intangibility, then, a movie is a process congealed into a thing; the theater is a process or performance that remains fluid and open-ended. As Susan Sontag has pointed out, films age; they are like cars or books or other consumer goods that grow old because they have a determinate reality. Stage plays, on the other hand, are always new, always take on a fresh existence; in Sontag's words, they "can only 'modernize.' "[117] When a second version of a film—with new actors, a different director, possibly a different setting—is brought to the screen, we refer to it as a "remake," as though it were the updating of an artifact. The original artifact may satisfy us more or less than the new model does, but in any case it continues to exist. The comparable term for the theater, "revival," implies a bringing back to life of something that has ceased to be and that can live only in performance.[118]

This contrast between the two media is analogous to the distinction made earlier between cinematic "being" and histrionic "doing," between the movie as autonomous entity and the play as fugitive action. And here, again, in the matter of generic durability, culture colludes with national bias. The drama's mutability intersects with the English love of tradition, with the verbal transmission down the generations of arcane ceremony and custom. The fixedness or being of film is American in that it minimizes the motivation to remember. In its objecthood, the genre has a closer relation to novels and poems than do the stage plays Cavell lumps together with those arts. Film is really the modern equivalent of print, not orality, and discussions about it—to reinvoke my earlier Puritan analogy—are like colloquies about scriptural passages, not about perishable sermons. American nonchalance about getting the past right accords with the tenor of motion pictures because the mechanical reproduction the cinema shares with printed literature supersedes memory instead of mobilizing it.

American modernity has invariably announced itself as a preference for the legible. Not the embodied, and not the invisible either, but the permanently readable. In part this is a democratic impulse, underwritten by impatience with personalized authority. Countless illustrations from the national canon come to mind, but perhaps none is more revealing than the self-originative gesture of that ur-American, Benjamin Franklin, as related in his *Autobiography* (1793). (It is no accident that Franklin, the first "representative" American, was a printer as well as a revolutionary and self-made man.) Franklin devotes several pages to describing how he learned to write effective prose. At first his father Josiah took him under his tutelage, reading Benjamin's essays and pointing out infelicities in expression and argument. Shortly afterward the young man happened upon an issue of *The Spectator*:

> I thought the Writing excellent, and wish'd if possible to imitate it. With that View, I took some of the Papers, and making short Hints of the Sentiment in each Sentence, laid them by a few Days, and then without looking at the Book, try'd to compleat the Papers again, by expressing each hinted Sentiment at length and as fully as it had been express'd before, in any suitable Words, that should come to hand.
>   Then I compar'd my Spectator with the Original, discover'd some of my Faults and corrected them.[119]

What leaps out at once from this passage is the disappearance of the father. Franklin, having committed himself to the world of books and print, to the first modern cultural technology, can relinquish the older generation without regret. Having started out by deferring to the wisdom of another man, he ends by doing away with flesh and blood altogether and apprenticing himself to a thing. The printed text contains all he needs to know in order to master the knack of elegant writing; it renders the father's skills, and the father himself, superfluous and obsolete. Books empower self-sufficiency. They undermine the past as a living presence, and they reduce reliance on memory. Who needs to keep esoteric information in one's head when it can be obtained from the printed page? Who needs to cherish the past when the accummulated wisdom of the ages can be distilled between the covers of a book?

American mistrust of memory is deeply egalitarian, just as English regard for the faculty has elitist implications. Knowledge locked up in memory, to the democratic mind, is knowledge that cannot be scrutinized. It shrouds itself in secrecy and exclusion. Eighteenth-century Americans, in establishing their republic, insisted that the elementary principles of free government be made accessible to all in a written document. The English, whom the Founders accused of seeking to enslave them, had an unwritten constitution; its precepts were not readily consultable as a check on arbitrary rulers. (To this day the movement for expanding individual liberties in Britain takes the form of a demand for a written bill of rights.)

To know the principles of their federal constitution, and to exercise the suffrage in an enlightened fashion, Americans had to read and write. By the nineteenth century, when the franchise was still severely restricted in Britain, and many ordinary subjects received no schooling at all, Americans could boast of the most thorough system of common schools anywhere in the world. The English may have had the ablest novelists, but to prosper they had to sell their wares across the Atlantic. The largest literate population in history was found in the United States, almost 90 percent of the adult whites in 1850. American egalitarianism, to be sure, stopped at the bar of color; black slaves couldn't vote, and in southern states it was illegal to teach them to read and write. Class did the work of race in England. Even some Britons who favored popular literacy opposed teaching writing to the lower ranks. The poor needed to read to make sense of orders from their superiors; they had no reason to write because they had no orders to give.

American egalitarianism, understood as the subordination of selective and auratic oral forms to universal and repeatable "print," has persisted in the cinema and climaxed with the VCR. Home video equipment is the culmination of film's break with live theater's hierarchies and cult of memory. It has taken roughly a century for this technological upheaval, or, alternatively, this Americanization, to become complete. On the actor's side, however, the devaluation of remembering set the screen apart from the stage from the beginning. The man or woman playing the lead role in a West End production had (and has) to commit hundreds of lines to memory. Silent film players didn't have to memorize any speeches at all, and they needed to learn by heart only a general outline of their physical movements: positions before the camera could be choreographed aloud by the director while the scene was being shot. With sound, players have to remember the words assigned to them, but few actors are obliged to master more than a handful of lines each day. And as great a film star as Marlon Brando has built a career on never memorizing the daily script; he counts on the spontaneity of his reaction to his part to carry over into the finished picture.

The film actor, then, evinces an intuitively American presentism; liberated from the need to remember, he has only to "be" himself in order to succeed on celluloid. Contrastingly, the stage performer requires an

English deference to history; he has to "do" the work of memorization in order to learn his part and realize his dramatic character.

## Monarchs and Actors

Bagehot, turning his beacon on the executive function in the English constitution, differentiated between the monarch as the dignified or ceremonial side and the prime minister as the efficient or active element. The monarch, on this division, had a theatrical role to perform and was responsible, in the working of government, for

> that which is occult in its mode of action; that which is brilliant to the eye; that which is seen vividly for a moment, and then is seen no more; that which is hidden and unhidden; that which is specious, and yet interesting, palpable in its seeming, and yet professing to be more than palpable in its results.

Today's British monarch is a doer par excellence, but a doer, as Bagehot's account suggests, in the purely histrionic way I have described. The Queen, though perhaps a bit more than a figurehead, is anything but "free" to do as she might like; her political actions issue not from her convictions but from the requirements of her station. She fulfills her position as monarch by acting the part assigned to her by history and convention, and above all by signing the bills passed by the Commons; she has no power to veto or amend. As Bagehot puts it, "She must sign her own death-warrant if the two Houses unanimously send it up to her."[120] Bound to a script, which she executes with staid aplomb, Queen Elizabeth (like Victoria before her) is exemplary of her subjects, the model even in a post-royalist age for the self-advertised English strength of "doing one's duty." Her children and in-laws, but especially her sons, have fallen in popular estimation in proportion to their failure to perform their roles with comparable proficiency.

Granted, the Queen does not rule; that "efficient" part is carried out by the prime minister in combination with the cabinet and the

Commons. But the retention of the monarchy as the premodern and theatrical half of the executive expresses something distinctive about English culture, something for which there is no equivalent in the government of the United States. Or rather, the president, whose power is both symbolic and actual, comes nearest to being the American counterpart to the monarch. And how could one omit mentioning that the United States capped its long flirtation with the cinema by anointing a film star, Ronald Reagan, as fortieth president?

The choice is as pregnant with meaning as the British deference to the Crown. Not by chance did Reagan triumph electorally at the head of a movement to restore free-market merit to preeminence in American culture. He operated in the political domain much as he did as an actor in the cinematic world; he embodied individualist self-identity by playing the part he was best at playing, which was himself. Reagan first made a virtue of his political amateurism when he ran for the governorship of California. His handlers, seeking to divert criticism of his ignorance on many issues, touted him as the antithesis of a professional, a citizen-politician who had no more specialized knowledge than the average Joe but whose vision—anti–big government, pro-self-reliance—could reinvigorate the state.[121] Reagan never forgot the formula. He was the amateur as president, the man from outside the Beltway who lacked the insider's answers but had the instincts of an ordinary American. While others have adopted the antiprofessional tactic, few have played it as flawlessly as Reagan did, and his Hollywood background was ideal preparation for the part. Like the movie actor he had been, he wasn't an expert or a polymath; he was always and only himself.

Reagan's ascension to the presidency gave another kind of boost to the symbiosis between American cinema and politics: it accelerated the packaging of electoral campaigns as motion pictures and of candidates for office as movie stars. (Which could also be construed as the reduction of the public sphere to mass entertainment.) If, as the saying has it, politics is show business for ugly people, Reagan's good looks and sensitivity to his effect on viewers blurred the already faint line between the two realms and made the promotion of national leaders as much a matter of polling and audience approval as the marketing of blockbusters.

There is, in fact, some ambiguity about which locale, Washington or Los Angeles, borrowed the other's methods. Dick Morris, President Bill Clinton's disgraced consultant, claims to have learned his polling strategies from the selling of movies. But campaigning for office was the major public spectacle of the nineteenth century, and John Gregory Dunne has suggested that politics gave the idea of tracking polls to Hollywood. "Opening a big-budget film," says Dunne, "bears certain similarities to running a national political campaign. Everything is geared to polling, and then taking the polling results and targeting a broader audience base."[122] Reagan's facility in navigating the two professions was the earnest of their growing indistinguishability.

## English Movies, American Theater

To assert a greater or lesser degree of proficiency in a cultural idiom is in no way to imply either a monopoly or a vacuum. The British have made outstanding films, and Americans have sparkled at all phases of the drama. But British cinema, as I observed about *Shallow Grave*, is recognizably different from its American counterpart, closer in some respects to the stage than to the usual Hollywood product. It is cinema, but it is also *British*. Conversely, the theater of the United States often seems a near relative of the motion pictures. The typical Broadway show, like its cinematic neighbors down the block at Times Square, can feel worlds apart from the highly literate, classically acted entertainments of the West End. Here, again, nationality is as much the operative category as genre is.

Few would dispute the rapport between English movies and English plays. The similarities begin with the sharing of plots and actors. Britain's top performers, unlike American movie stars, are comfortable shuttling between the two arts, and Britain's filmmakers are enamoured of their theatrical heritage. They shoot Shakespeare's plays in particular with a panache that Hollywood used to lavish on westerns. And British dramas and motion pictures alike thrive on a diet of great novels, finding sustenance in classic works by Austen, Dickens, Brontë, Fielding, Defoe, and Forster.

Convergence with the stage describes a cinema that has muted the medium's "Americanism." English movies tend to be less expensive than American ones, less action-oriented, more spatially restricted, and more cerebral and articulate (hence elite). Two hits of 1996, *Secrets and Lies* and *Trainspotting*, show far greater sensitivity to language than Hollywood fare. Institutional history and philosophy reaffirm the evidence of deviation on the screen. From its origins in the second industrial revolution, the British film industry has trailed in the efficiencies of advanced capitalism. It long maintained an artisanal resistance to certain divisions of labor: as late as 1912, an American visitor expressed disbelief that the tasks of producing and directing were still concentrated in a single person. Vertical integration of the manufacturing, distributing, and exhibiting processes was also slow to catch on. Nor did British companies canonize individualist values to the same degree. The Ealing studios, instead of encouraging competition among writers or producers (the norm in Hollywood), established creative groups working together. It was famous as "the studio with a team spirit." A more collaborative outlook prevailed among performers too. The English did not set up an equivalent of the Academy Awards to salute actors for outclassing each other.[123]

America's commercial theater, in contrast, has mitigated the form's "Britishness" by interpolating qualities frequently thought of as cinematic. Arthur Miller (not, to be sure, a disinterested party) has argued in a number of critical pieces for a view of the United States drama as more attuned to mass taste than the European variety. Our plays, Miller says, are more kinetic, less long-winded, and less addicted to paradox and verbal glitter. "Put simply, we write plays for people and not for professors or philosophers; the people abroad accept and love many of our plays, and in some cases, even the philosophers do too."[124] While Miller's brief might be dismissed as special pleading, other, more neutral witnesses have also found Broadway less intellectual and more physicalized than the London stage.[125] If Eugene O'Neill's *The Hairy Ape* (1922), with its violent, atavistic protagonist, could only have been written by an American, Tom Stoppard's wordplay and philosophical fluency specify

*Arcadia* (1993) as unmistakably a work of the English imagination (in this case, an English imagination of Czech pedigree). One might further note, a bit facetiously, how often American dramatists have been entangled with Hollywood. Miller's own marriage to Marilyn Monroe is a notorious example; but not to be forgotten are Edward Albee's adoption by the film magnate, Reed Albee, and Sam Shepard's second career as a movie star.

Although all these illustrations are taken from the twentieth century, the strongest proof of a filmic Broadway precedes film's existence. The most significant area of American distinctiveness is acting: the preoccupation with authenticity or "being," which I discussed earlier in relation to the motion pictures, actually has its provenance in the stage and is as much a feature of the American theater as the movies. Drama critic Robert Brustein, who is now head of the American Repertory Theater, considers this emphasis on selfhood the curse of our performing arts:

> Reflecting his interest in the self, the American actor usually purveys a single character from role to role, one that is recognizably close to his own personality. This subjective, autobiographical approach to performance is reflected in the most prominent American acting method where the current jargon includes expressions like "personalization" and "private moment," signifying techniques with which to investigate one's own psychic history.

Brustein blames the prestige of such self-involved techniques on the Actors Studio, which conflated inarticulate muttering with acting in the forties and fifties "through a mistaken reading of Stanislavski."[126]

Whatever one may think of them, Brustein's strictures misidentify the lineage of American stagecraft's embrace of self-expression. The passion for psychological authenticity stretches back to well before the Actors Studio. Puritanism, with its soul-searching and public confessions of sinfulness, would be one possible source, coterminus with the New World's settlement; another possibility, this time dating from the age of revolution, would be republican ideology. Rousseau, whose dread of the theater's corrupting influence was limitless, felt that the institution could not be permitted in a free state because it made a cult of imposture. Thus it opened the door to demagoguery. What, Rousseau asked, is the actor's profession? "It is the art of counterfeiting himself, of putting on another character than his own, of appearing different than he is, of becoming passionate in cold blood."[127] A style of acting that renounced dissemblance, that substituted frank self-revelation for two-facedness, would be, if not acceptable to Rousseau, at least arguably a democratic improvement.

Some version of this attitude lay behind the partisanship aroused in the mid-nineteenth century by Edwin Forrest, the athletic American theater star, and William Macready, his more refined English rival. Forrest, the darling of the groundlings, was a staunch Democrat whose acting technique supposedly reflected his egalitarian politics. His perfervid and exhaustive style aimed for paramount emotional effect in order to woo the popular audience. Forrest labored to abolish the distance between his own persona and his parts (which, indeed, were written expressly for him in playwriting competitions that he sponsored). Florid gestures, hortatory address, and appeals to heaven, the staples of Victorian melodrama, were used to achieve the same self-expression as Method minimalism. Whether in the role of Metamora, or Spartacus, or Jack Cade, three star vehicles that became synonymous with the actor, it was always Edwin Forrest who paced the boards and poured out his soul in passionate gushes for his public.[128]

Erwin Panofsky, among others, has said that film, unlike the stage, establishes a "consubstantiality" between performer and character: Richard III survives Olivier or Branagh, but Terry Malloy "lives and dies" with Brando.[129] Forrest's example shows how this merging could occur in the antebellum American theater. Macready, Forrest's English rival, put a good deal less stock in self-display. He was an aspiring gentleman who preferred drawing-room restraint and played, as it were, the stage actor to the American's movie star. Study alone, Macready liked to say, could ensure competent acting; sincerity was never enough. In phrases that evoke nothing so much as finishing school, the Englishman spoke of the need to pay "strict attention to one's elocution, deportment, gesture, and countenance." Macready wanted to expunge rowdyism from the pit no less than from the stage. He insisted that education and taste were quite as essential to appreciate good acting as they were to produce it.[130]

The feud between these two men has been remembered because it was a precipitating factor in the bloodiest theater riot in American history. In 1849 the actors, then both appearing in New York City, scheduled separate performances of *Macbeth*. Forrest's backers, decrying Macready as an aristocrat and regarding his aloof acting style as an insult to American patriots, stormed the Astor Place Opera House where he was performing. A full-scale riot ensued, and the militia was called out to restore order. It dispersed the mob by firing point blank into its midst, leaving twenty-two rioters dead and another hundred and fifty wounded.

We will see later that this tumult antedated the high Victorian's theater's mutation into movie-palace-like passivity. What convulsed Astor Place, it might be said, was an exhibition of participatory democracy in action, the kind of audience involvement (carried to excess, of course) that marks today's London playhouses. But the fact that Herman Melville, no foe of democracy—he was about to compose *Moby-Dick*—signed a petition on behalf of Macready should give us pause. (Melville may have modeled his autocratic Captain Ahab on Edwin Forrest.)[131] It may be that the huge Jacksonian theaters (seating capacity, 3,000 to 4,500), combined with the adulation showered on actors like Forrest, fostered not genuine participation but something like that demagoguery Rousseau was so afraid of. One historian of the riot, Bruce A. McConachie, has concluded as much. McConachie believes that Forrest's charismatic persona reduced his auditors to quiescent (if explosive) malleability. His performances of swashbuckling warriors bred "authoritarian hero worship, not democratic empowerment."[132]

Even in the nineteenth century, in other words, the acting philosophy later identified with the movies ("Be yourself") may have contained an imperial element, an inducement to submission, that did not become fully manifest until the ascendancy of Hollywood.

## Realism, Nature, and the Frontier

The 1890s, date of the cinema's nativity, were synchronous on this side of the Atlantic with two far-reaching historical developments. The decade brought the official closing of the frontier—announced by the Census of 1890 and publicized as an ominous national watershed by historian Frederick Jackson Turner in his address of 1893—and it saw the Republic's emergence as a global and imperial power, successor to Spain's dominions in the Philippines and Latin America. Historians like to remark on the linkages between the last two events. The vanishing of territory or empty space within the continental boundaries, goes the argument, fed the appetite for space and markets without. Less has been said about the cinema's place in this particular historical conjunction. Yet the movies too bear the traces of their originary moment.

For the present our concern is with film's position as a "new frontier," as the medium was hailed in its infancy, a compensation or redress for, and an accommodation with, the wrenching thrust into post-agrarian modernity.

Turner had identified American democracy with the adventure of settling the land, and in his famous address he implied that freedom might be in danger with the frontier's disappearance. His worries were widely shared. Many Americans felt disquiet over the apparent evaporation of the country's special bond with the physical environment, its privileged standing, in a favorite nineteenth-century phrase, as "Nature's nation." As cities swelled from internal and external immigration, people's contact with the natural world diminished. Exchange and mediation, spectacle and information—in a word, the regime of vicariousness—replaced direct experience. Teddy Roosevelt decried the loss of hardihood in native stock and proposed "the strenuous life" of travel and exercise as a remedy. The conservation movement, with Roosevelt's support, campaigned to preserve our natural heritage. And in literary art, the catchword was realism, the faithful imitation of natural appearance.

In this climate, the movies appeared like a deus ex machina offering the promise of recuperated nature. The silver screen would restore connection to reality—indeed, would afford unprecedented access to the natural world. Things never seen before by the human eye—such as the growth of a flower, compressed into seconds—could magically be observed inside dark rooms in the heart of concrete cities. No matter that the filmed images were silent, that they were colorless, that they flickered, that they moved faster or slower than real life, and that the screen was flat and squared off at the edges. This was reality in motion, hurtling trains and waves breaking upon shores, produced for viewer titillation with a fidelity that no painting, photograph, or playhouse could approach. Even the real itself, according to some, couldn't outdo the visual literalness of the cinema:

> Edison's latest marvel, The Projectoscope. The giving of life to pictures so natural that life itself is no more real.
>
> Life motion, realism, photographed from nature so true to life as to force the observer to believe that they [sic] are viewing the reality and not the reproduction.[133]

Reality it wasn't, of course, but the eagerness with which Americans seized upon the illusion is worth attending to. American film could have taken other directions than it did, developed other identities than the classical Hollywood style and its hyperrealistic progeny. Not all movies have adopted such illusion-fostering techniques as indirect address, on-location filming, and naturalistic acting. Miriam Hansen has shown that primitive pictures regularly shattered the self-contained diegesis by direct looks at the audience and by the retention of nonfilmic features like lectures and vaudeville acts.[134] In Europe, antirealism blossomed from the beginning. The best-known early French filmmaker, the fantasist Georges Méliès, told stories about the man in the moon and had decapitated characters scurry about in search of their heads. In the United States, we use the term *cinematic* to mean, among other things, vivid and panoramic; in France, "c'est du cinéma" means "that's phony."[135] Expressionism has flourished in Germany at least since 1919, when Robert Wiene directed *The Cabinet of Dr. Caligari*. Bertolt Brecht's ideas for epic theater and the disruption of dramatic realism were partly inspired by the experimentation of the movies.

The American tradition has been very different, far closer to Ibsenite naturalism than to Brechtian innovation. This is not to say that all Hollywood films have been realistic. But the tradition has embraced, rather than tried to subvert, its technological *donnée*, the use of the camera to record the visible, the photographic accuracy of the moving image. Its objective has been the Conradian one, as paraphrased approvingly by D. W. Griffith in 1913, "above all to make you see." American film has striven for "the redemption of physical reality," in Siegfried Kracauer's words, and given its viewers what the French screenwriter Jean-Claude Carrière calls "essence of world, canned and bottled."[136]

While it may well indicate good business sense for Hollywood to have made a cult of realism, the disposition is also a product of the national longing for proximity to nature. The cinema's rise in the era of the frontier's passing gave that desire a particular authority in American popular entertainment that it has never relinquished. The movies have been the twentieth-century successor to the wilderness as the quintessentially American "thing," the defining attribute of the culture and the guarantee of American at-home-ness in the actual.

But it has been argued previously that holding onto nature is more characteristic of the English, with their theater and live actors. It might further be objected that America's defining cultural achievement in the current century lies elsewhere, in the antinaturalism of its glass-and-steel skyscrapers or in the fine arts. In painting, the United States has been at the forefront of abstract expressionism. This circumstance presents us with a paradox, but not, I would contend, a contradiction. Americans crave realism and nature, but usually not in unmediated form; they have wanted the wilderness "conquered," the frontier "tamed," and the physical world improved upon. The cinema has prospered in this country because it imports antinaturalism into mass culture under the cover of nature. It employs technological means to bring the visible universe under human mastery. In the movies, as Umberto Eco has written of California (in the aptly titled *Travels in Hyperreality*), "Absolute unreality is offered as real presence."[137]

Some final words about comparative attitudes toward the natural environment. English coexistence with the physical world is a product of both history and topographical inheritance. Britons were keen on subduing the earth until the end of the eighteenth century, when they began to appreciate their island for its animals and scenery.[138] A century later, many Americans came to the same conclusion about their surroundings. But except for the weather (and American extremes are unknown), nature in England presents a less intimidating face to humanity. To encounter towering mountains, vast deserts and prairies, and surging rivers, one has to travel across the Channel or the Atlantic. In the United States, nature throws up formidable obstacles to human will, and although Americans identify with their grander physical environment, for most of their history their relation to the continent has been more adversarial than accepting. American movies resolve this dilemma: they pay tribute to the natural and simultaneously abolish it.

### Aside on Stephen Crane

Crane's fiction, a literary high point of the 1890s, is a revealing early instance of film's impact on the novel. Unlike the initial wave of American realists, William Dean Howells, Henry James, and Mark Twain, all of whom were born decades before the Civil War, Crane was young enough—barely twenty-two when *Maggie: A Girl of the Streets* appeared in 1893—to take account of cinematic discoveries. He was one of the first to grasp, and to interrogate, the extent of the infant medium's cultural ambitions.

In *Maggie*, the proscenium arch, boundary marker between the observed spectacle and the observing audience, has disappeared; or, perhaps more accurately, the frame isolating the scene of action from the viewer has strayed outside the theater and now encloses the world as a whole. Crane subjects Victorian melodrama, with its pretensions to "transcendental realism," to merciless satire, showing it to be an utter falsification of the experience of slum dwellers like his protagonist, Maggie Johnson. The play Maggie sees with Pete, her brutish suitor, centers on a "hero's erratic march from poverty in the first act, to wealth and triumph in the final one."[139] Nothing could be less like Maggie's own transit from poverty to sweat shop to prostitution and suicide.

The movies are the paradigm for heightened verisimilitude and for the erasure of the dividing line between stage and real life. Crane's novella, duplicating and even anticipating the cinematic revolution, gives us "the world in a frame" (to appropriate the title of Leo Braudy's book on film). Maggie, Pete, and the other characters become the objects of spectatorship themselves, their behavior relentlessly scrutinized by neighbors, strangers, and the reader. The disgraced heroine is ogled by Rum Alley onlookers, staring "as if they formed the front row of a theater"; her mother gestures at her "like a glib showman"; and as Maggie walks the docks where she drowns herself, the very buildings are said "to have eyes" (61, 68).

What Crane refuses to accept is the notion that the camera achieves greater naturalism by extending the stage's dominion. There is no outside anymore, he indicates instead, no place where the real can hide from the reign of surveillance. In representing modern life as a society of the spectacle, Crane exposes the fallacy that the movies, or any other art, can enjoy a privileged access to the unmediated actual. The novella ends with Maggie's death and with her mother putting on an exhibition of grief for the assembled "spectators." As the scene nears its climax, Crane writes that the "inevitiable sunlight came streaming in at the windows and shed a ghastly cheerfulness upon the faded hues of the room" (73–74). *Everything* is artificial now, including nature itself: reality is another name for illusion, for the quotidian rendered theatrical by the very fact of its being watched.

It is a relevant detail that not long after publishing *Maggie* and his best-known novel, *The Red Badge of Courage* (1895), Crane served a stint as a correspondent during the Spanish-American War. He might thus be described as the poet laureate of American imperialism. Richard Harding Davis, his principal rival in reporting the Cuban campaign, believed that Crane "easily led all the rest" in the freshness of his writing. Crane, who had tried to enlist in the Navy before signing up with Joseph Pulitzer's *New York World*, an organ of "yellow journalism," basically endorsed the American policy of occupation. The United States was not an imperialist power, he explained in an interview with a London paper; the Cubans would be granted their independence when "they have grown to manhood." The sole proviso was that the little island ("only ninety miles distant from the United States") keep its "sluice gates opened," for Crane was, "of course, a Free-trader," and he considered it his country's right to have the run of the native market.[140]

A possible bond between the cinematic imagination and the American strategy of indirect empire will be examined shortly in this essay; what should be remarked on here is how Crane's brand of realism is imbued with imperialist logic. His is an art of expansion. Taking as his motto the Shakespearean adage that "all the world's a stage"—the motto put into practice by the cinema—he reaches out in every direction, enfolding the spectators, the street, the sunlight, and construing them all as actors and scenery. Crane's realism engulfs the world, finding a frame wherever it turns: persons become performers; action, acting; and the whole of human life a movie.

## Richard Chase and the Exceptionalism of American Culture

Forty years ago the critic Richard Chase published an influential study of *The American Novel and Its Tradition*. Chase's argument was that the literature of the United States had diverged from its English parent. The "American novel" was actually a romance genre; it shunned the prosaic realism of social fiction for abstractness, symbolism, and the heightened effect. Whereas the traditional novel preserved a connection to our daily lives, romance severed the tie between imagination and actuality. It carried fictive invention to extremes that surpassed anything we could know as social creatures. Chase cited as exemplary the words of two American authors—Henry James on the representation of "disconnected and uncontrolled experience," and Herman Melville's statement that readers want "nature . . . ; but nature unfettered, exhilarated, in effect transformed."[141]

Chase's analysis has been criticized for slighting more earthbound American subgenres like the domestic novel, and at first blush it would seem to have little relevance to the movies, which, as has been emphasized, were born in the age of realism. But if the fit is not perfect, neither is it far from the mark. The cinema's disruption of the space and time continuum, perhaps the fundamental experience of moviegoing, approximates the romance condition of "disconnectedness," just as the stage's propinquity to the theatergoer evokes the relatedness of the social novel. In the drama, events and characters are "hypothetical," but they are present to us. We can reach out and interfere in what is happening. Film viewers have no such access to the represented universe; they can neither enter nor touch the doings on the screen. The movies, to quote James again, confront us with the things "we never *can* directly know."[142] They construct a world that is literally elsewhere.

And a world that is radiant with meaning. Film, like the romance genre, invests the physical environment with connotational richness; it abounds in symbolic objects. *Rosebud* is the medium's scarlet letter or white whale. Moreover, the cinema delivers a vision of the actual that is both superrealistic and utterly fake. Its images are oversized and incandescent, its characters larger than life, its plots crammed full of impossible actions. Faux nature, nature exaggerated and transfigured, ties together the fictions of James Fenimore Cooper, the films of Martin Scorcese, and the composition tennis courts at Flushing Meadows.

## History Lessons
### Imperialism, the English Stage, and American Movies

"The sun, it appears, never sets on the British empire and the American motion picture."[143]

Mention the words *imperialism* and *Hollywood*, and people automatically mouth the adjective "cultural." With good reason. The movies, aping the role of whiskey and religion in the nineteenth century, have been at the vanguard of American capitalist penetration. The figures can be staggering. The United States, which produces a tenth of the world's pictures, collects two-thirds of the global receipts. Today over 80 percent of European box office revenues are for American films—this on the continent of Jean-Luc Godard, Federico Fellini, and Sergei Eisenstein. The monopoly was almost as great in the 1920s, and Hollywood began its international conquest even earlier, with the breakthroughs of Porter and, above all, Griffith's *The Birth of a Nation* in 1915.

But even these numbers are not adequate to convey the extent of American filmic dominance. Hollywood movies dwarf local products in box office income in almost all the world's nations. In Japan, seven of the top ten grossing pictures in 1995 were American-made, including the first six. In Germany, Turkey, and Poland, Americans supplied nine of the top ten. And in Australia, Brazil, Chile, Egypt, Switzerland, Hungary, and Great Britain, the United States swept the cinematic board, claiming all ten of the top earners.[144] (India, with its mammoth native film industry, is the exception to American domination.)

The specter of audiovisual dictatorship, unlike the specter of communism in Marx's famous manifesto, is not a hallucination but a truism of international life. Rational people warn darkly of European cinema expiring before the onslaught of Hollywood filmmakers.[145] The British motion picture industry is one of several that have tried to defend themselves against the New World invasion. Acts passed by Parliament in 1927, 1938, and 1947 sought to limit foreign imports by establishing quotas for domestic production. A percentage of all movies exhibited in England had to have a British author, be filmed in British studios, and employ British labor. But nothing could stop the American offensive, and the chief result of the protectionist legislation was the so-called "quota quickies," technically inferior films made on the cheap to beef up indigenous output.[146]

Britain, at least, has been spared conquest and occupation in this century and so has preserved the nominal right to keep out American products. But after World War II, much of the rest of Europe had no choice—and even Britain's options were more hypothetical than real. The Hollywood monopoly was backed by United States government muscle. Under the terms of the Marshall Plan, the shattered societies of Western Europe had to show American movies or else lose the foreign credits they desperately needed in order to rebuild. Films exported to Germany, once a major competitor to Hollywood, were subsidized by Marshall funds in the amount of $25,000 per picture.[147]

The Hollywood juggernaut would be an obvious way to talk about the movies and imperialism, but for our purposes it wouldn't be the most revealing. Of more interest here is what America's cinematic ascendancy suggests about the complex interrelationship between types of entertainment and trajectories of empire. The discussion in this section takes off from a series of significant concurrences: American movies and American overseas expansion, arising in near-tandem with one another, also coincided with the final spasm of British world dominance. As the Union Jack beat a protracted retreat before American triumphalism, so the stage and the screen evolved different, almost antithetical, characters. The two art forms have reproduced, or, it may be, facilitated, the reconfiguration of the two people's global influence.

As a first step, we need to return, not to the moving picture's debut, but to a point even further back in time, the period before the cinema, the middle decades of the nineteenth century. And we immediately encounter an unexpected discovery: the drift toward impersonality and self-enclosure, which we have taken to be characteristic of the cinema, originated in the drama. Before (roughly) the 1860s or 1870s, English plays were marked by a high degree of performer/audience interaction, anticipating the communal spirit evident today; but in the years between, and particularly toward the end of the century, the stage embraced the distance and heightened artifice that became the signature of the movies.

Most spectacularly, riots and other violent outbreaks occurred with some frequency into the early years of Victoria's reign (1837–1901). (A similar level of turbulence roiled the American stage, climaxing in the infamous Astor Place Riot of 1849, but shown also by lesser disorders in Boston, Baltimore, and Philadelphia, and by an earlier New York brawl, the Farren Riot of 1834.)[148] But more meaningful than these extreme incidents were the accepted rules of theatrical attendance. Foreign visitors expressed astonishment at the lack of decorum inside London playhouses. Auditoriums, illuminated by candles or gas, were never dark, the spectator sitting in full or only partially lowered light, and animated conversation continued throughout the performance.

The English themselves seem to have relished such irreverence, or at least to have regarded the informal ambience as one of the theater's chief attractions. Michael R. Booth, a historian of the Victorian stage, quotes an observer who fondly described the sensation of being "in the picture, beholding, yet part of it." Stages extended into the audience, and actors coming downstage to speak their lines found themselves in close proximity to the patrons in the pit in front of them and in the boxes on either side. "The spaces in front and behind the footlights seem to blend," another contemporary remarked. Acting style was melodramatic, and responsive to the public's wishes. In the "point," the actor would advance to the front of the stage and declaim directly to the audience; enthusiastic applause could inspire him or her to repeat the speech numerous times.[149]

This participatory ethos became a casualty of Victorianism. Ossification was a gradual and uneven process, but for convenience's sake we can pick a single year as the turning point—let us say, 1876, the date of Victoria's crowning as Empress of India. By then, or not long after then, the old traditions were being abandoned. Theaters grew darker in decoration and lighting, the modern habit of blacking out the house and fixing all eyes on the stage originating as early as 1859.[150] Hubbub gave way to respectful attention, intimacy to spatial partition. Actors could no longer physically approach the audience because of changes in stage design. Forestages contracted until they became flush with the proscenium, and a gilded border framed the scene of action. The performer was now confined within a picture frame, with the theatergoer observing the picture from outside.

New methods of acting reinforced the sense of invisible boundaries. The "point" couldn't survive the proscenium arch, and actors began to behave as though the audience were the fourth wall of a room, addressing all words and gestures to each other and betraying no awareness that they were being watched. The classical Hollywood practice of indirect address—the injunction never to look at the camera—preceded Hollywood's existence; it was an innovation of Victorian stage managers.

Decor underwent similar changes. Scenery, once minimal, now aspired to three-dimensional verisimilitude; sets grew ever more detailed, effects more spectacular. Henry Irving, the great English actor-director (who was knighted in 1895, the first thespian considered respectable enough to receive the honor), used distinguished painters like the Royal Academy's Lawrence Alma-Tedema to achieve photographic accuracy.[151] The objects that fill today's silver screen, mesmerizing audiences with their lifelikeness, originally appeared on London's stages. Blizzards raged, waterfalls cascaded, and live animals trooped across the boards. Early Victorians knew they were attending plays; late Victorians required the illusion of reality—of a world independent of them, which they could observe but not affect.

Booth sums up these developments by saying that they "well suited the growing passivity and detachment of the Victorian middle-class audience."[152] We can ascribe the changes, as is customary, to the era's investment in propriety and self-control. We can also note, on the American side of the water, a hierarchizing of public culture that corresponds to increasing social stratification.[153] But still another explanation is the one I wish to pursue here: not by chance did the hardening of barriers between audience and representation take place in theaters named, according to the fashion prevalent during this period, to advertise Great Britain's international might: the New Cross Empire, the Birmingham Empire Palace, the Sheffield Empire Palace, the Empire Theatre, Leicester Square, the Edinburgh Empire Palace, and on and on, in every corner of the land.

Taken together, the combination of naturalist autonomy, audience exclusion, and imperial showcase points to a dovetailing of politics and entertainment. While the drama was being transformed into inviolable spectacle, England was busy consolidating its position as the world's foremost power. The British tightened their grip on Asia (Burma was finally conquered in 1885–86); gobbled up huge portions of Africa, including Egypt, Kenya, Ghana, South Africa, and Rhodesia (the European powers formally recognized these colonial divisions at the Berlin Conference of 1884–85); extended their reach into the Mediterranean, where they acquired Malta and Cyprus; and denied Home Rule to Ireland until after World War I.[154] Government may have become more democratic at home, through enlargement of the suffrage, but power and its prerogatives were being redefined globally as something exercised by an ever smaller number of people, situated at a distance from those they ruled. Decision-making was supposed to flow in one direction, from the epicenter to the margins. The masses were expected to look on, and the colonized to submit to orders over which they had no control.

The provisionality of these statements is deliberate. Although power in its imperial distribution may have been hypothetically monologic, in practice it was polymorphous. The colonial authority could dictate policy but not always govern reception; the colonized found ways to evade, frustrate, and oppose distant orders even while appearing to comply with them.[155] By the same token, the masses in the metropole nurtured their own forms of resistance to the centralizing of command. They could curtail power's freedom to operate by their sullen or withheld obedience. But on the whole the English populace went along with geopolitical developments. All classes, including the economically precarious, "passively acquiesced" in the solidifying of national prestige. The music halls where jingoism reigned were a working-class phenomenon and often bore the same name, "Empire," as their theatrical betters, the legitimate playhouses of the West End.[156]

In form, then, the late Victorian theater aped the imperial dynamic. The drama's restructuring had the effect of quarantining important action. Everything that mattered transpired on the other side of the footlights, behind a border no member of the audience could overstep. Spectators at the New Cross Empire might applaud, or they might refrain from applause, but no longer did they intervene in what was happening.

Although we might denominate the new arrangements as "cinematic," intending the term to encompass passivity and noninvolvement, the description wouldn't be entirely apt. The early American moviegoers studied by Hansen and others were not the docile, regressive spectators of French cinematic theory. In the 1890s, films were commonly screened on vaudeville programs; after about 1905, neighborhood nickelodeons became the chief exhibition outlet. The men and, in large numbers, women who packed these theaters came from the working class. Many were immigrants, and they relished the picture shows in part for their interactive atmosphere, which included songs, lectures, and live acts.[157] The nickelodeons were at the cultural antipodes from the West End, and from Broadway; arguably *more* participatory than the high Victorian drama, even with its human actors, they tore down the wall separating the public from the performative space.

Yet within a decade, Hollywood had more or less adopted the classical grammar. By 1915 or so, nonfilmic accompaniments had been

exiled from the movie houses, which redirected their appeal to the affluent middle class. Realistic, self-contained narrative was now the desired
form of entertainment, and indirect address replaced the conspiratorial
wink at the audience. American cinema, in short, quickly eclipsed the
theater as a locus of the inaccessible; simultaneously, the United States
started to elbow aside the British as a player on the world stage. The
Crown instituted "Empire Day" after a costly victory in the Boer War
(1899–1902), but Britain's imperial fortunes, as Teddy Roosevelt
declared in private, were "on the downgrade." American power, by way
of contrast, was in the ascent, and dramatically so. The United States
annexed the Philippines, Puerto Rico, and Hawaii; effectively seized
control of the Panama Canal; and asserted authority over Latin and
South America with the Roosevelt Corollary to the Monroe Doctrine
(1904).[158]

All these triumphs were in the service of a brand of overseas expansion notably dissimilar from the British prototype: an imperial diegesis,
as it were, that recapitulated the national preference for film over the
drama. In thirty years of colonial conquest, Great Britain increased its
empire by almost five million square miles, until it possessed fully one
quarter of the earth's surface. Even in its imperialist heyday, the United
States added only 125,000 square miles. What Americans sought,
through the policy called "dollar diplomacy," was not land but markets,
outlets for the mountains of goods produced by their farms and facto-
ries. The British desired markets, too, but believed they had to rule foreign peoples in order to ensure commercial access. Americans did not
physically vanquish alien societies; they were content to extract guarantees of openness to trade.[159] Mimicking the movies, they chose mediation over presence, and they built a "virtual" empire that has outlasted
the concrete but vulnerable one established by the British.

One might even say that open markets, the rallying cry of the emergent imperium, supplied the rationale for cultural form as well. The
turn-of-the-century American economy, historians agree, suffered
repeated downturns owing to overproduction. "Free-trade" expansion
promised an antidote to business cycles: foreigners would buy the
excess products that would otherwise rot in warehouses. The movies
likewise offered relief from economic distress. They would eliminate the

glut of goods by inducing Americans themselves to increase their level of consumption. Film's incomparable glamorizing of material objects constituted a marketing bonanza as effective in its way as the prying open of Chinese or Nicaraguan ports.

The classical cinema's first major success, Griffith's *Birth of a Nation*, made all too evident the medium's imperial cast. The picture was shown at regularly stipulated intervals and at prices as high as $2.00, in a deliberate repudiation of the nickelodeon's working-class sociability. But the real target of Griffith's laudatory film about the rise of the Ku Klux Klan was not a class; it was the black man. Griffith took as his theme the coming together of North and South at the expense of a nonwhite race's rights. This was the national reconciliation, signaled by the end of Reconstruction in 1877, just one year after Victoria's naming as Empress, that had established the basis for the United States's entry into global politics.[160]

Griffith's cinematic melodrama rivaled in vaulting ambition the theaters in which the classical movies were played. The unassuming nickelodeons had lasted less than a decade, and from 1914 through the early talkies most Americans watched their picture shows in palaces as imposing as the most majestic British "Empire."[161] (It is suggestive that these extraordinary buildings began appearing on the threshold of World War I, a still European-centered conflict that was to make America's might plain to all. The intervention of United States forces in 1917 turned the tide of battle against Germany and ensured victory for the Allies.)

Samuel "Roxy" Rothafel's Strand, in New York City, with a seating capacity of three thousand, is usually regarded as the first of the deluxe theaters. Contemporary newspapers understood at once that the ornate, intimidating edifice was meant to convey a message about power: they compared seeing a film there to attending a reception at the White House. The movie houses that followed in the Strand's wake were replicas of European and Oriental palaces. They combined ornamented facades with opulent lobbies and vast auditoriums, some, like New York's Radio City Music Hall, able to accommodate as many as six thousand patrons. Designers ransacked foreign countries for old paintings and antiques to decorate the foyers and promenades. Among the most renowned imitation palaces were Grauman's

Egyptian and Chinese, both of Los Angeles, the Oriental in Milwaukee, the Regent Theater in Manhattan, with an exterior modeled on Venice's Palace of the Doges, and the Aztec Theater in San Antonio, Texas.

The movie palaces tended to be Asian and Spanish in atmospherics; that is where the United States had its empire, in the Pacific and Latin America.[162] A few theaters were explicit about their collusion with "manifest destiny." The San Antonio Majestic replicated the Alamo down to the chapel-fort's bells. And many theaters, even in the North, practiced internal segregation, restricting blacks to (the inferior seating in) the second balcony. White supremacy at home complemented imperialism on foreign terrain. The African American going to see *The Birth of a Nation* at the nearest palace would be treated, in setting and on the screen, to the same exhibition of racial hierarchy that colored peoples abroad experienced in their daily encounters with white colonialists and traders.

Hollywood films introduced those alien peoples to American sights and consumer goods; they also brought the world to American audiences. In both respects, the motion pictures collaborated with the imperial agenda. By laying the faraway and exotic before the spectator in Jersey City or Chicago, the cinema asserted a kind of proprietory title over the globe. And because the images projected on the screen were overwhelmingly American, the movies naturalized our realities as "normal": the sound Bell telephones make when they ring, the cars New York City police ride in, the way our homes and landscapes look.

This irreducible ethnocentrism belied the cinema's claim, much bruited in the medium's youth, to be a common language, understandable and communicable by every people. Laemmle called his studio Universal, and though the movies (before *The Jazz Singer*, 1927) were silent, promoters championed the art form as a visual Esperanto, ideal for articulating the all-embracing idiom of the emotions. But the cinema's idea of inclusivity denoted deference to American wishes, even to American racial prejudices. Revealingly, Thomas Dixon was among the first to use the universal formulation. Dixon was the North Carolina-born author of *The Clansman* (1905), the novel on which *The Birth of a Nation* was based; he set forth his understanding of the new "University of Man" in his unpublished autobiography, explaining that the movies would appeal to

> the dark skinned hordes of Abyssinia, the yellow millions of the Far East, the dreamers of India, the warriors of Islam, the hosts of Russia, Europe and the two Americas. . . . We can make them see things happen before their eyes until they cry in anguish. We can teach them the true living history of the race.

For Dixon, the truth about race ordained the subjugation of colored peoples by the white man. In his scenario, as in Griffith's finished picture, the disenfranchisement of the freedman presided at the birth of the modern United States.[163]

Americans have acted resolutely to ensure that theirs would be, if not the only, at least the dominant language heard, and the dominant image seen, in movie theaters throughout the world. At the outset of the twentieth century, Hollywood filmmakers conspired to expel French companies like Pathé from American markets; at the turn of the twenty-first, they haven't hesitated to enlist the government (as at the GATT talks) in their campaign to obliterate foreign production.[164] Such imperial designs, under the guise of millennial universalism, are by no means a novelty in United States culture. A literary scholar is reminded of Herman Melville's prophecy, in *Redburn* (1849), that "on the world's jubilee morning," the "curse of Babel" shall be revoked, and the language all humanity shall speak shall be English.

## Excursus
### The Fifties and the Cold War

Allied success in World War II ensured the United States of first rank among the world's nations. The war left Germany and Japan in ruins, and Britain at the end of its career as an imperial power. Only a weakened Soviet Union remained to contest American supremacy. Yet the euphoria of being number one was short-lived, as it quickly became evident that the postwar years would be a time of abnormal tension and fearful responsibility. International leadership, ostensibly a cause for self-congratulation, in fact filled many Americans with disquiet.

The imperial regime was palpable in American popular culture, where spectacle and optimism set the tone. The movies of the 1950s were marked by bold technological strokes, the advent of stereo and widescreen projection, and by enthusiasm for costume sagas in which Christianity took the field against a tyrannical Rome. These pictures replayed some of the preoccupations first aired in the British "toga dramas" of a half century earlier. On the popular stage, the Broadway musical or "New York Opera," as it has been described,[165] laid brief claim to theatrical superiority. But in entertainment, much as in politics, surface impressions were misleading. Behind the swagger of Cinerama and of blockbusters like *Ben Hur* (1959) lay gnawing doubts, apprehensions about democratic betrayal aroused by the Republic's assumption of the imperial crown.

The major innovation in postwar film was the expanded screen format promulgated in various guises between 1952 and 1955. Departures from the narrow 35mm standard had actually been in existence since the medium's birth. Wide-film systems had failed to catch on in the 1890s; a second flurry of experimentation in the twenties, capped by Abel Gance's three-camera Polyvision, also met with rejection from the public. Increased screen size didn't win popular approval as a norm, rather than a distracting novelty, until the introduction of Cinerama in 1952, to be followed in rapid order by 3-D, CinemaScope, and Todd-AO. (The expanded screen or anamorphic process is now the industry standard in the more modified form of Panavision.)

Why did widescreen gain acceptance in the fifties? The leading scholar of the process, John Belton, notes that outdoor recreations like hiking and boating were now available on a mass scale. These more participatory leisure activities conspired with their opposite, television in the home, to lure viewers away from the movie theaters. The film industry set out to recapture its lost clientele by satisfying new appetites for grander, more involving entertainment. Promotional literature for enlarged-size cinema emphasized its ability to draw spectators into an illusory world and to overwhelm them with ultrarealistic sound and images.[166]

Global events also contributed to widescreen's acceptance. Spectacular cinematic effects complemented America's emergence as the planet's foremost superpower. The change in the nation's self-conception from the interwar period, when isolationist sentiment ruled politics, was nothing less than astonishing. The United States, though never renouncing its belief in "free-trade imperialism" nor hestitating to intervene militarily in Latin America, had refused to join the League of Nations and adopted a series of Neutrality Acts forswearing entanglement in foreign affairs. Two decades later, international commitment had become an accepted fact of life. The nation deployed the first atomic bomb, occupied Germany and Japan, rescued Europe from starvation with the Marshall Plan, and, by the 1950s, had assumed the position of world's policeman. American troops were battling Communism in Korea barely five years after Hitler's defeat; Eisenhower made peace in 1953 but authorized overt or secret operations in Guatemala, Iran, and Lebanon.[167]

Wide-film exhibition was both a literal product and a figurative celebration of America's new-fledged world dominance. Fred Waller, the inventor of Cinerama, developed the technique's direct precursor in World War II to train aerial gunners for combat against enemy fighters. Brian O'Brien, the optical scientist behind Todd-AO, made an even bigger contribution to postwar hegemony. He helped build the ultra-high-speed camera used to photograph test explosions of the A-bomb.[168]

Awesome visual spectacle evocative of imperial prowess characterized widescreen from the start. The format's commercial debut, *This Is Cinerama* (1952), displayed stereotypical scenes from foreign lands and natural wonders of the United States. Touristic samplings of a Spanish bullfight and an Italian opera were overshadowed by dizzying aerial sweeps of the Grand Canyon and Niagara Falls. According to the *New York Times*, President Eisenhower was so stirred by these images that he "sang aloud the words of 'America the Beautiful' and 'The Battle Hymn of the Republic' as the music was played during the motion picture."[169] Subsequent examples of widescreen, both documentary and fictional, struck the same note of patriotic grandiosity. Cinerama specialized in travelogues that vindicated the slogan of Cook's Tours: "The World Is Yours." In *Cinerama Holiday* (1955), a sightseeing excursion through

Europe concludes with a Fourth of July fireworks exhibit in New England. The medium extended its scope (and American technological flair) into outer space, as it traversed the farthest quarters of the universe in *2001: A Space Odyssey* (1968). The marvel of 3-D entered the widescreen fray with *Bwana Devil* (1952), and Todd-AO shattered box office records in 1958 with *Around the World in Eighty Days*. Other titles, produced for propaganda use, were screened at world trade fairs to demonstrate American superiority over the Soviet Union.

These fifties spectaculars were the American equivalent of the British Empire melodramas of the 1890s. The stage plays had offered guided tours into the exotic realm beyond the nation-state, safely exposing London audiences to the customs and locales of subject peoples. British "excursion" dramas flourished alongside the expanded opportunities for travel organized by the original Thomas Cook, who had served the Empire by arranging transport for the British army in Africa. The dramas, like their equally flag-waving cinematic progeny, echo the insight that knowledge is the handmaiden of imperial power. As Edward Said has pointed out, information about alien cultures, however slanted, confers the conviction of mastery over them.[170]

A second group of films to make their mark on the enlarged screen were religious epics. Although the fad for stories of primitive Christianity predated widescreen by several years—Mervyn LeRoy's *Quo Vadis* came out in 1951—the genre took off with CinemaScope's inaugural feature *The Robe* (1953), starring Richard Burton and Victor Mature, and included the hits *Ben Hur* and *King of Kings* (1961). Again, the prototype for these pictures was not so much the American cinema as the British stage. Toga dramas, typically centering on the conflict between imperial Rome and Christ's fervent early disciples, had been immensely popular at the end of the nineteenth century. Perceiving the Roman Empire as a parallel culture, English theatergoers relished the plays as a testing ground for their own concerns about national decay and renovation.[171]

It need hardly be said that such themes resonated with special force at a time when American piety was at a pinnacle and the main threat to national prestige came from "atheistic Russia." Religion in the fifties presented itself as the only reliable safeguard against foreign aggression and domestic subversion. The phrase, "one nation under God," was added to the Pledge of Allegiance; church membership attained levels never equaled again in the century; and revivalists like Billy Graham enrolled the Deity in the struggle against Communism, which he believed to be a conspiracy hatched by Satan. "If you would be a loyal American," Graham exhorted, "then become a loyal Christian."[172]

The Bible epics staged the Cold War as a historical costume drama, with the Kremlin in the role of pagan despotism and the United States identified with Christianity. When Cecil B. De Mille prefaced his 1956 production of *The Ten Commandments* (which cast the Egyptians as the ancient persecutors) with the questions, "Are men the property of the state? Or are they free souls under God?," moviegoers not only knew the answers; they knew the relevance to the present. In *The Robe* a fiery Richard Burton, playing the tribune Marcellus, is converted by the garment Jesus wore at the crucifixion. Though Christ's Kingdom is not of this world, Burton tells the Emperor Caligula, it will vanquish Rome's "aggression and slavery" through the omnipotence of faith.[173]

The movies of the fifties, then, foregrounded the medium's imperial confidence; but the same movies were sensitive to Cold War strains and contained a second message. In the effort of widescreen to deny its cinematic identity, postwar film hinted at a profound discomfort with the informal American Empire's concentration of power and policymaking. Todd-AO in particular tried to counteract widescreen's penchant for pyrotechnical effects; it encouraged, if not the reality, at least the impression of a kind of democratic involvement.

The international front had been the first to lose its glow for Americans. Disenchantment began with the very fact that there *was* a Cold War, and that Russia had hardened into a superpower adversary within moments, so it seemed, of V-E Day. When the Soviets exploded an atomic weapon in 1949, they effectively negated the oceans as the guarantee of American security. The arms race was the consequence, with Truman giving the go-ahead for development of the hydrogen bomb. A year later the North invaded South Korea and American soldiers found themselves in combat once again, in an undeclared war that cost fifty thousand lives and resulted not in victory but in apparently endless stalemate. Peace, when it came, offered scant relief from imperial worries. Eisenhower's secretary of state, John Foster Dulles, devised the policy of massive retaliation, which meant that a handful of officials could have plunged the whole of humanity into a third—and, in its devastation, final—world war.

On the domestic side, the "warfare state" produced great prosperity but equally great assaults on civil freedoms, as fear of Communism infected government and culture. The Truman administration instituted loyalty oaths and arrested the Rosenbergs for espionage, but to the demagogic Joe McCarthy the Democrats themselves were guilty of "twenty years of treason." McCarthy burst into prominence in 1950 with accusations that the State Department was infiltrated by Communists. Bureaucrats, movie actors, and college professors lost their jobs in the ensuing hysteria. Disliked but tolerated by Truman's Republican successor, McCarthyism remained an intimidating force in public life until the senator's censure in 1954.

As early as 1946, Dean Acheson, then undersecretary of state and later Dulles's equivalent under Truman, had caught the anxious spirit of the age. The world's problems, he warned, "will stay with us until death. We have got to understand that all our lives the danger, the uncertainty, the need for alertness, for effort, for discipline will be upon us. This is new for us. It will be hard for us."[174]

Acheson's first-person plural underlined the felt need of American leaders to dispel the suspicion that decision-making after Hiroshima was monopolized by an elite few. Widescreen lodged a similar bid for inclusion by rhetorically replacing stationary spectatorship with active participation.

Publicity campaigns for the wide-film process hammered home this selling point. The wraparound, horizontal picture, reinforced by stereo sound, was so graphic, so lifelike, according to the ads, that viewers were lifted out of their seats in the darkened auditorium and swept into the action. "Everything that happens on the curved Cinerama screen is happening to you. . . . You share, personally, in the most remarkable new kind of emotional experience ever brought to the theater." Wide film refused to concede immediacy to live plays; its promoters insisted that the giant images had overcome the movies' traditional limitations and achieved parity with the drama as a medium of presence. Todd-AO ads went so far as to allege that the improved pictures were not movies at all. ("You won't be gazing at a movie screen . . .") Instead they were "shows," a third species of dramatic entertainment that combined cinema's visual grandeur with the experiential quality of the London or Broadway stage. "Suddenly you're there," blared the program booklets for the 1955 film of *Oklahoma!*, "in the land that is grand, in the surrey, on the prairie! You live it, you're a part of it . . . you're in Oklahoma!"[175]

Of course, no more than in the case of Acheson's "we" did such participation really occur: the literal contiguity of space between observer and scene of action that distinguishes the drama was purely illusory with Todd-AO. But the extravagance of the claim for this most extragavant of cinematic spectacles suggested the degree of popular concern over diminished agency. So strong was the cultural desire for input that widescreen productions *preceded* the English stage in valorizing audience engagement; they anticipated by several years the creative ferment instrumental in restoring London to theatrical leadership. I will turn shortly to the drama; here I want to note that the sense of threat addressed in Todd-AO's marketing strategies could also be found—muted, to be sure—on the level of theme. The wide-film epics that arrayed the "Evil Empire" of Russia-Rome against the "Good Empire" of America–primitive Christianity were not immune to the fear that the two empires did not, in the end, differ all that much.

Twentieth Century-Fox's *The Robe* illustrates the idea. As indicated previously, the film observes the toga formula rather closely. It tells the story of a Roman tribune's acceptance of, and indoctrination into, the new religion, of his love for a highborn Roman woman (Jean Simmons), who also embraces Christianity, and of their joint refusal to disown their faith when faced by death. Drenched in didacticism, *The Robe* is full of solemn speeches and anthemlike music, as well as the kind of portentous statements cherished by the religious epics: when Victor Mature asks if the Jewish messiah is God, a Roman soldier responds enigmatically, "He is, but he isn't." English actors, scions of the most recent obsolete empire, were much favored for the roles of Romans; it is perhaps significant that Mature, who is an American and plays Burton's Greek servant, survives to carry on the struggle.[176]

The King's Head Pub, on Islington High Street, houses a thriving theater.
PHOTOGRAPH BY THE AUTHOR

The Hackney Empire, built 1901. One of London's last surviving "empire" theaters, now fallen on hard times.

PHOTOGRAPH BY THE AUTHOR

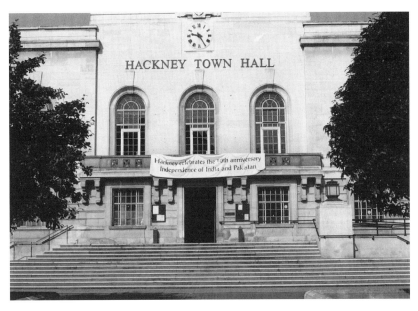

The Hackney Town Hall, down the block from the Empire, commemorates the
fiftieth anniversary (1997) of Britain's passing as an imperial power.
PHOTOGRAPH BY THE AUTHOR

The Elphinstone Picture Palace, Bombay, India. Successor to the empire theaters, this movie palace in Britain's "crown jewel" colony has the look of a temple. Note the native drivers.

AUTHOR'S COLLECTION

Shakespeare's Globe, rebuilt on London's Bankside. Communitarianism redivivus?
Or Shakespeareland come to the big city?

London's weekly guide
April 23-30 1997 No.1392 £1.70

**Time Out**

20-page film special

Hollywood

London

Why Tinseltown can kiss our feet

The 25 most powerful Brits in LA
Donna McPhail parties in Soho
London's black vote: exclusive poll

The London edition of *Time Out*. Fantasies of the British movie
industry supplanting Hollywood.

AUTHOR'S COLLECTION

(COURTESY OF LONDON'S WEEKLY ENTERTAINMENT GUIDE, TIME OUT)

Louis B. Mayer (*center*, in pin-striped suit), the Russian-born Jewish movie mogul who claimed that his birthday was the Fourth of July. Irving Thalberg stands at Mayer's right.

AUTHOR'S COLLECTION

The transition from communal space to the inviolate enclosure of the proscenium
is well under way in this 1888 newspaper drawing of the interior of the Royal
Court Theatre in London's Sloan Square.

HARPER'S WEEKLY

A JOURNAL OF CIVILIZATION

Vol. XLII.—No. 2179.
Copyright, 1898, by Harper & Brothers.
All Rights Reserved.

NEW YORK, SATURDAY, SEPTEMBER 24, 1898.

TEN CENTS A COPY.
FOUR DOLLARS A YEAR.

COLONEL THEODORE ROOSEVELT, U.S.V.

The paladin of American overseas expansion, Teddy Roosevelt of the Rough Riders,
on the cover of *Harper's Weekly*, September 24, 1898.

American "free-trade" imperialism contrasted to the landgrabbing rapacity of the European powers. Cartoon by W. A. Rogers, from the cover of *Harper's Weekly*, November 18, 1899.

Grauman's Chinese movie palace.
AUTHOR'S COLLECTION

[ABOVE] D.W. Griffith's vision of heaven in the 1915 print of *The Birth of a Nation*. Paradise for whites only.
AUTHOR'S COLLECTION

[BELOW] An American flag replaces the heaven sequence in the 1933 "Collector's Edition" of *The Birth of a Nation* "produced under the personal supervision of D. W. Griffith."
AUTHOR'S COLLECTION

D. W. Griffith

"You live it, you're a part of it...You're in Oklahoma!" Shirley Jones and Gordon MacRae in the widescreen production of *Oklahoma!* (1955).

Imaginative conquest of the globe in Todd AO's *Around the World in
Eighty Days* (1958).
AUTHOR'S COLLECTION

Denzel Washington in his Oscar-winning performance as the runaway slave Trip in
*Glory* (1990). Washington was the only black film actor to crack "The Top Forty" in
show business salaries for the combined years 1995 and 1996.

AUTHOR'S COLLECTION

What complicates this straightforward scenario is the last third of the movie, in which Burton/Marcellus is taken prisoner and brought before the Emperor Caligula for questioning. The vaguely effeminate dictator, ranting against "a secret party of seditionists," resembles Joe McCarthy as much as Joe Stalin; the state he ruthlessly administers could as easily be the Red-scare United States as the Soviet Union. (The screenplay for *The Robe* was written by Philip Dunne, a liberal who spoke out against inquisitorial trampling on defendants' rights and was himself blacklisted.)[177] Caligula conducts the trial as a parody of an investigation by HUAC (House Committee on Un-American Activities), the Congressional committee that had targeted Hollywood "subversives" in a 1947–48 dry run for McCarthyism. Doubling as judge and jury in classic witch-hunter fashion, he demands that Marcellus renounce Jesus and swear allegiance to Rome. Somewhat unexpectedly, Burton kneels and takes his loyalty oath to the state; while he admits to being a Christian, he explains to the tyrant that he cannot be a traitor because Jesus "seeks no earthly throne." (One feels a certain sympathy for the skeptical Caligula during this exchange: the followers of the new faith clearly do desire the Empire's downfall.) The hero is martyred anyway, a victim of intolerance for dissent.

*The Robe*'s ideological inconstancy places it in a complex relation to the venerable American practice, tracing back to the War for Independence, of reading contemporary politics in terms of ancient Rome. Revolutionary leaders, steeped in the classics, would don togas to declaim against oppression. But the Rome they had in mind was the Republic; their British foes symbolized the Empire. Condemning America itself as the Empire didn't gain currency until the 1890s, and the negative use of the analogy predated the occupation of the Philippines: the most famous example is probably Ignatius Donnelly's Populist novel, *Caesar's Column* (1890). To Donnelly, the United States was a bloated, selfish giant, a latter-day Roman plutocracy in which a handful of capitalists lorded it over the "writhing masses." *The Robe*'s creators manage to have it both ways: imperial Rome is enemy and self, at once Communist totalitarian behemoth and anti-Communist security state.

Before shifting focus to England, it will be instructive to glance at the contemporaneous Broadway scene and at the outpouring of "popular opera" that established this country's brief claim to be the capital of the theater world. According to the cultural historian John Dizikes, the native musical achieved its greatest success in the two decades between 1940 and 1960, exactly as the United States embarked on its rise to superpowerdom. Dizikes regards *Pal Joey*, the 1940 collaboration of Richard Rodgers and Lorenz Hart, as the launching of the phenomenon. After Hart's death in 1943, Rodgers teamed up with his more famous partner, Oscar Hammerstein II; together they composed such classics as *Oklahoma!* (1943), *The King and I* (1951), and *The Sound of Music* (1959). Other triumphs of the period included Kurt Weill's *Lost in the Stars* (1949), Frank Loesser's *Guys and Dolls* (1950), Frederick Loewe and Alan Jay Lerner's *My Fair Lady* (1956), and Leonard Bernstein's *West Side Story* (1957).[178]

As the names listed above make clear, Dizikes's designation "New York Opera" is a euphemism for "Jewish Opera": the one area in which Broadway indisputably trumped the West End was, like the movies, the handiwork of Jews. (Weill's 1935 decision to migrate to New York instead of London merely underscored the cultural benefits of American receptivity.) That the musical's heyday was roughly coeval with the breakthrough of wide film is no accident: both stage and screen dazzled audiences with visual and aural spectacle, mounting elaborate, costly productions commensurate with national ascendance. But just as the widescreen epics resisted their own autarchy through the "participation effect," so the musical as a genre flouted the strict boundary-policing of representationalism. The popular opera may have aspired to accurate costumes and settings, but its conventions are the antithesis of realist self-enclosure: music and dancing disrupt absorption in the narrative flow. Moreover, the fact that songs are constitutive of the form's identity guarantees a measure of audience involvement. Who can leave a performance of *Oklahoma!* without humming "Oh, What a Beautiful Mornin'," thus in a small way adding one's voice to the occasion? Significantly, when the British moved to reassert their histrionic primacy, in the wake of Empire, they abandoned the spectacle side of theater altogether and concentrated their energies on deconstructing the circumscribed diegesis. (Bertolt Brecht, whose Berliner Ensemble sparked the English revolution, was himself the author of "musicals."

He theorized a function for song and dance as shattering psychological naturalism. Brecht's songs have been recorded by David Bowie, Sting, Jim Morrison, Bobby Darin, and other pop artists.)[179]

## History Lessons (Continued)

The English themselves have pursued a less triumphalist cultural and political program than their now full-grown American progeny. In dramatic art, the first glimmerings of a new spirit were already visible in the 1890s. These hints of change came not from the English or even the European epicenter but from the continent's margins, and they can be taken as harbingers of the twentieth century's colonial uprisings, the eruption of agency from the subaltern peoples of the periphery. The Irishman George Bernard Shaw, the Scandinavians Henrik Ibsen and August Strindberg, and the Russian Anton Chekhov all mounted assaults on the calcified Victorian stage (though all, to varying degrees, continued to prize psychological realism). Shaw tried as valiantly as anyone to jolt London theatergoers out of their cordoned-off complacency. He published an appreciation of Ibsen in 1891, praising the Norwegian for "making the spectators themselves the persons of the drama," and he wanted his own social problem plays to force the audience "to face unpleasant facts." (His first three works carried the unapologetic title *Plays Unpleasant.*)[180]

A second wave of change, beginning with the new century and lasting into the 1920s, issued directly from Shaw's Irish homeland. Its point of origin was Dublin's Abbey Theater. The leading experimenters included William Butler Yeats, J. M. Synge, and Sean O'Casey, and they too broke away from Victorian protocols in their use of artifice and open staging. But the mainstream English theater refused to follow these leaps forward. The West End was to remain locked in proscenium-arch naturalism for years, until the cultural ferment of the provinces, spilling into politics, reached the capital as revolutionary demands for independence.

The dismantling of the Empire under colonial pressure began in earnest with Ireland and Egypt. Cairo won its autonomy in 1922, and in the same year the Irish Free State was established, although national sovereignty for Eire (as the republic was named) within the British Commonwealth had to wait until 1937. Not until after World War II did Britain's unseating as superpower by the United States become an international commonplace. Exhausted by six years of bloodshed, spared conquest itself only by American intervention, Whitehall reluctantly accelerated the decolonization of its outposts in Asia, Africa, and the Caribbean. India, the heart of the Empire, was granted freedom in 1947; Burma and Ceylon (Sri Lanka) in 1948; Ghana in 1950; and the West Indies in the 1960s.[181]

The long and enervating battle against the Axis had bred a sense of common purpose among the English. As imperial grandeur faded, the conviction grew that society had a duty to protect the welfare of all its members, regardless of income or rank. The election of 1945 installed the first majority Labor government in Britain's history, and with it acceptance of the idea that the state should be responsible for unemployment insurance, public assistance, and medical care.[182]

Many felt that the theater, as a treasured English institution, had a vital service to perform in the nation's rejuvenation. John Maynard Keynes, mastermind of the welfare state, was named the first head of the Arts Council, an organization set up in 1946 to provide government support for culture. The goal of this initiative was to create an environment, modeled on the Elizabethans, where artists and the public would sustain one another.

Keynes's manifesto, "The Arts Council: Its Policy and Hopes," rewards scrutiny as a pivotal document in the history of the English stage. Its prejudices are undisguised: pro-live entertainment, anticinema, anticultural imperialism. Summoning his readers to rebuild English "common life," Keynes homed in on the movies as a threat to theatrical survival no less deadly than the Nazi onslaught. The chief obstacle to reestablishing the performing arts in Britain, according to him, was the shortage of suitable buildings: "Of the few we once had, first the cinema took a heavy toll and then the blitz." Keynes conceived of the drama as an agency of decentralization, the antithesis of the cinematic monolith. He wanted to encourage regional theaters and to demolish the imperialism of the metropole, by which he meant both London and the United States:

How satisfactory it would be if different parts of this country would again walk their several ways as they once did and learn to develop something different from their neighbours and characteristic of themselves. Nothing can be more damaging than the excessive prestige of metropolitan standards and fashions. Let every part of Merry England be merry in its own way. Death to Hollywood.

Keynes's almost agrarian nostalgia, so manifest (and chauvinistic) in this passage, was equally transparent in his subordination of mediated, impersonal performance to live exhibition and player-audience intimacy. While he praised the BBC for broadcasting concerts to millions of music lovers during the war, he regarded listening to the radio as mere training for the "enhanced excitment and concentration of attention and emotion" involved in hearing an orchestra in person and "being one of a great audience all moved together." Nothing can compare with "the living performer and the work of the artist as it comes from his own hand and body, with the added subtlety of actual flesh and blood." Keynes concluded his hymn to immediacy and fraternity with the hope that the Arts Council would earn a place for postwar Britain in "the great ages of a communal civilized life."[183]

Keynes's extraordinarily condensed summary of English cultural objectives was not to bear full fruit for over a decade. Its vision of renewed common life crystallized in the drama as a final repudiation of Victorian rigidities and a steady movement toward the collaborative credo of today. Joan Littlewood of the Theatre Workshop spearheaded the English branch of the revolution (joined somewhat later by the English Stage Company's George Devine), but the key figure wasn't a native of the U.K., and the critical moment didn't occur until 1956. That was the year when Brecht's Berliner Ensemble journeyed to London and electrified the theatrical establishment with antinaturalistic plays featuring "alienation effects." Equally significant, 1956 was the year of the Suez crisis, when the United States forced the British to back down from their latest (and practically their last) imperial adventure.

The current London theater is a legacy of this historical concatenation. The "Empire of the Stage" (as denominated by the magazine *Vanity Fair*) is post-imperial, skeptical of authority and determined to undo the prohibitions barring the audience from involvement. Until Tony Blair's election, it was an oppositional theater, mounting resistance not to the British Empire, which is long defunct, but to the imitation imperial government of conservative reaction, and to the American leviathan that loomed behind the return to laissez-faire. The renovated English drama acknowledges its roots in the postwar welfare-state consensus. Its adversary has been the pseudo-American sentiment, enunciated by Thatcher in a free-market delirium, that "there is no such thing as society, only individuals and their families." Against American atomism, love of the modern, and naturalistic storytelling—against, in a word, the movies— the theater proclaims its self-conscious allegiance to custom and community, its residual humanism in a society of the spectacle. My visit to the King's Head was emblematic in ways I couldn't then imagine: the performance within the pub was the counterpart to the protest outside, dual manifestations of disaffection from England's takeover by American values. One can only wonder how the London theater will evolve under a Labourite adminstration that copies Washington's economic policies and rejects socialism more decisively than it does Thatcherism.

## Annus Mirabilis: 1956 [184]

I have already commented on some of the events crowding into this year and making it, on balance, the most noteworthy modern date in theatrical/cinematic history. (The much-discussed 1890s remain my choice for the seminal decade.) England, no longer master of its own fate, experienced humbling in Egypt by its American ally and the renovation of its stage from Germany. The United States had its destiny confirmed as the free world's paladin to the Soviet Union's tyrannical empire: in a single year, Khrushchev managed both to disavow Stalin's legacy, in his secret attack at the Twentieth Party Congress, and to refurbish that history of repression by dispatching Russian tanks to quash the Hungarian uprising.

Nineteen fifty-six ushered in two milestones for the cinema, though they fronted in contrary directions. Film's status as a machine-produced vendible experience, rather than a material good, became the pacesetter for the whole economy. For the first time in the country's history, more Americans were employed in service and white-collar occupations than in worker-type jobs producing things.[185] The service side of the economy, with Hollywood as the bellwether, has never looked back. By 1992 the United States enjoyed an unrivaled superiority in telecommunications and entertainment. The country ran a $96 billion deficit in goods, but had taken over first place as a global service supplier: its surplus in that sector was 56 billion dollars.[186]

By a strange irony, the videocassette shared its birthdate with the inaugural eclipsing of things by services. The movies, facing stiff competition from television and outdoor recreation by 1956 and suffering falling revenues at the box office, took their first step toward evolving into a novel-like, home-based, physical commodity. The Ampex VTR (videotape recorder) was introduced at the National Association of Broadcasters convention in Chicago. This forerunner of home video, an American invention, was developed for mass dissemination by the Japanese; within a decade, Sony and Matsushita dominated the market for VCRs.[187]

It exaggerates somewhat to lay the 1956 revival of English drama to Brecht's epic theater; Littlewood and Devine deserve credit, and above all so does John Osborne, who was discovered (by Devine) in that year and had his *Look Back in Anger* produced at the Royal Court Theatre in Sloan Square. But Osborne's early career actually underscores the importance of Brecht's influence (and of the Suez crisis) in transforming the London stage. *Look Back in Anger*, for all its "kitchen-sink" realism and vehemence against the class system, is in many respects a conventional play. A proscenium arch safely encloses the action, and the plot has been compared, not unfairly, to a soap opera.[188] Osborne's characters exude a frustrated air of having been bypassed by the world's great events. They spend their time reading the papers instead of doing anything memorable. (The one-room flat in the Midlands groans under its weight of newspapers and weeklies.) Colonel Redfern, Alison Porter's father, has returned from India to find his country as diminished as he is; according to a stage direction, his authority, like England's, "has lately become less and less unquestionable." Jimmy Porter, the "angry young man" protagonist, speaks ruefully of England's decline: "it's pretty dreary living in the American Age—unless you're an American of course." Change and purpose in Osborne's picture of postwar society seem always to hover offstage.[189]

A few months later, after Suez and the Berliner Ensemble, aesthetic revision and global upheaval have moved to the foreground and are tangible forces in *The Entertainer*. Although the play was first performed (again at the Royal Court) in 1957, Osborne wrote it in 1956, and the action occurs during that pivotal moment. *The Entertainer* heralds in its unorthodox achievement the resurgence of the English theater, at the same instant that it explores as its theme the collapse of British power, symbolized by the decline of that popular institution, the music hall ("the local Empire"),[190] and by the downward spiral of Archie Rice, the obsolete "entertainer" of the title (originally played by Laurence Olivier). At the heart of the play is the death of Archie's son Mick, a soldier captured at Suez who is executed by the "bloody wogs." Mick's death occasions the despairing reflection that a century of imperial sacrifice has been an utter waste, all "for the sake of a gloved hand waving at you from a golden coach." Osborne reserves some of his harshest criticism for the idea, as expressed in a song about "good old England," that "We're all out for good old Number One,/Number One's the only one for me." It is a Thatcherite sentiment, twenty-five years before Thatcher. Osborne was himself to drift politically rightward and to accept much of the Conservative program. But in 1957 he treats Archie's theme song ("Why Should I Care?") as anathema to the communitarian emphasis of the music hall, which, he says, "is dying, and, with it, a significant part of England."[191]

Spurred by Brecht's innovations, Osborne attempts to preserve some of the music hall's spirit in his own play. *Look Back in Anger*, he admitted, had been "rather old-fashioned."[192] In the new work, he experiments with an episodic structure (thirteen short scenes) and with a cabaret style blending music and dance and including direct apostrophes to the audience. According to a prefatory note,

> I have not used some of the techniques of the music hall in order to exploit an effective trick, but because I believe that these can solve some of the eternal problems of time and space that face the drama-

tist, and, also, it has been relevant to the story and setting. Not only has this technique its own traditions, its own convention and symbol, its own mystique, it cuts right across the restrictions of the so-called naturalistic stage. Its contact is immediate, vital, and direct.[193]

Osborne's play punctures the membrane of the proscenium frame. It establishes an antirealist intimacy that looks ahead to the stagecraft of today.

In the United States the closest parallel to Osborne's cultural reformation was a movie rather than a play. *Rebel Without a Cause* screened at drive-ins and downtown palaces while *Look Back in Anger* was jolting Londoners at the Royal Court. The film addressed many of the same themes Osborne's work dealt with—aimlessness, disaffection from society—and it also centered on an angry young man, played by James Dean. England's moment of change launched the career of a playwright; America's, finding expression in the motion pictures, established Dean as a male movie star with the drawing power of Marilyn Monroe.


## A Note on Brecht and the Cinema


None of this is to say that Brecht's aesthetics had no impact on the movies. The German actively involved himself in films, and his legacy can be seen in the work of such compatriots as Alexander Kluge, Margarethe von Trotta, and Rainer Werner Fassbinder. Brecht also had a vogue among French filmmakers, especially in the aftermath of the revolutionary events of May 1968 (a good decade after the English stage's rebirth). His chief French disciple is of course Jean-Luc Godard, whose ventures in radical cinema include *Two or Three Things I Know About Her* (1966) and *La Chinoise* (1967).

But in the United States and Britain, Brechtian experimentation made little headway in the motion pictures. The anti-illusionism and spectatorial distancing that "took" in theater did not simply limp behind by some ten years in film; these techniques have had almost *no* influence in popular movies, and their adoption by Godard signaled his evolution into a coterie *auteur* with a steadily diminishing audience. In the early years of the post-studio era, hopes ran high among some critics of Hollywood for a personalized, alternative cinema. Instead Hollywood recovered as the ever more monopolistic and superillusionary production center of the blockbuster.[194] A few directors, notably Spike Lee and Oliver Stone, have retained touches of Brechtian self-reflexivity without greatly departing from the naturalist model.

Mainstream film, of all the mass media, has arguably proven the *most* resistant to unmasking of its power. Recent studies of public image-making note that the movies, unlike, say, television, shun the parading of their own machinery that Brecht believed would dissolve the visual medium's magnetism. The networks' ironizing of their coverage of political campaigning, in which they comment on their reporting of "spin," has evolved into a kind of prime-time theater criticism. But self-referentiality at CBS or Fox hardly amounts to an endorsement of Brecht. It suggests nothing so much as the exhaustion and media colonization of the playwright's ideas. Calling attention to the fakery of the image not only fails to deflate the authority of the contrived effect; a good case can be made that exposure actually redoubles the mechanical image's fascination.[195]

## Black Bodies, Modernity, and the Cinema
### The Birth of a Nation

> There is no document of civilization which is not at the same time
> a document of barbarism.
>
> —
>
> WALTER BENJAMIN, "THESES ON THE PHILOSOPHY OF HISTORY"

The leisure to write court poetry rested on the exploitation of the peasantry. Fascist sympathizers have penned imperishable novels. The scandal of the motion pictures is their genesis in racism. Chronologically the most advanced of the arts, film has proved to be the most retrogressive in its collusion with color prejudice. In contrast to popular music, in contrast, indeed, to traditional forms like poetry and the novel, film resisted the interracial borrowing that has hybridized American culture in the twentieth century.[196]

Two—or better yet, three—white Southerners, Griffith, Dixon, and Woodrow Wilson, thrust the moving pictures into modernity by collaborating on *The Birth of a Nation*, Dixon as novelist/screenwriter, Griffith as producer/director, and Wilson as witting or unwitting publicist whose presidential stamp of approval certified the medium's respectability. (Wilson's praise for the film's historicity after its private showing at the White House—"my only regret is that it is all so terribly true"—resurfaced in advertisements and was mustered as a defense against criticism from blacks.)[197] *Birth* was the cinema's *Iliad*, its coming of age as a major contribution to Western aesthetics. With this masterpiece, a paean to white supremacy, the movies lined up against the strain of modernism that championed the primitive and interactive. Imperial and self-consciously highbrow, *Birth* disowned the regime of presence and thematized film's methodological uniqueness as the evacuation of physicality. Thus did the silver screen set itself up as heir to the technology of literacy from which blacks had first been excluded during antebellum slavery.

Of course the movies were not alone in affirming racial hierarchy. The erasure and/or subordination of black bodies on a national and international scale shadowed the cinema's originary phase. Significant dates on the American side of this global movement would have to include 1877, 1896, 1905, and 1912. During the first year, Northern Republicans agreed to withdraw troops from the former Confederate states in exchange for the presidency. This bargain, known as the Compromise of 1877, sealed the abandonment of the freed slaves.

Eighteen ninety-six brought the codifying of segregation in the Supreme Court decision of *Plessy v. Ferguson*. The doctrine of "separate but equal" ensured that white Americans—in the South by legal statute, in the North informally by economic divisions and gentlemen's agreements—would be spared the affront of black proximity.

The next date, 1905, consummated the reworking of the Fourteenth Amendment into a legitimation of laissez-faire capitalism. The amendment had been adopted after the Civil War to grant citizenship and its protections to all freedmen, defined as persons born or naturalized in the United States. But as early as 1873, in the *Slaughterhouse* cases, the Supreme Court had begun to whittle away at these guarantees. In 1905, with *Lochner v. New York*, the Court struck down state laws regulating hours and wages on the grounds that corporations were "persons" who could not have their liberties abridged under the Fourteenth Amendment. Thus the rights intended to safeguard African-American human beings were transferred to disembodied corporate entities. And the rights of the former slaves themselves were stripped away throughout the post-Reconstruction South. Poll taxes and literacy tests disenfranchised the black masses and effectively repealed the Fifteenth Amendment guaranteeing them the vote.

The final year, 1912, marked the capitulation of the federal government to racial stratifying. In a three-man race, with Taft and Roosevelt splitting the Republican vote, the Democratic ticket headed by Wilson swept to national victory. The executive branch was now the preserve of Southerners, and Wilson lost no time in getting out the message that blacks were unwelcome. He immediately implemented segregation as the official governmental policy of the United States.

The black bodies reduced to invisibility and excluded from public voice remained a galling irritant to angry whites, who responded to the provocation of color with murderous violence. "Race riots," in which armed mobs assaulted and slaughtered blacks, occurred in 1898 in Wilmington, North Carolina (the African-American writer, Charles W. Chesnutt, based his 1901 novel, *The Marrow of Tradition*, on this incident); in 1907 in the centerpiece of the "New South," Atlanta, Georgia (a contributing factor on this occasion was an incendiary stage production of Dixon's *The Clansman*); in 1908 in Lincoln's adopted city, Springfield, Illinois; and in 1916 in East St. Louis, site of the worst massacre of all, where hundreds of blacks lost their lives, many of them burned to death in their homes. Another three thousand African Americans perished in lynchings between 1888 and 1918, some, according to James Weldon Johnson, for crimes as ludicrous as "talking back" to white persons.[198]

White supremacy was the uncontested dogma of the reunified Republic; it was also the ideology of the European powers and of the proponents (and some foes, too) of American imperialism. Behind the

American entrance into the scramble for empire lay the belief that the "inferior" races of Asia, Latin America, and Africa were unfit for self-rule. As important as the wish for markets was the self-proclaimed moral duty of the Anglo-Saxon to govern and uplift the world's colored peoples. The racism inherent in this perspective, immortalized by Rudyard Kipling as "The White Man's Burden" (the title of his poem of 1899), was not confined to jingoists; many who rejected the imperial siren did so out of the same sense of racial superiority. White Southerners like "Pitchfork" Ben Tillman complained of their region enduring "this white man's burden of a colored race in our midst." Tillman opposed the annexation of the Philippines on the grounds that the United States could not absorb another ten million alien (and debased) beings.[199]

Europe, with Britain in the lead, also trumpeted the racial element of imperialism. As the white (not just Anglo-Saxon) nations of the metropole extended their tentacles into Africa and Asia, they increasingly came to justify their conquests as missions to lesser breeds, even to subhuman species. England's Lord Rosebery articulated the European position when he queried in 1900, "What is Empire but the predominance of race?"[200] The Berlin Conference called by King Leopold of Belgium a decade before the Spanish-American War parceled out Africa under the pretext of civilizing the "dark continent's" barbarous inhabitants. The civilizing process dragged on: as late as the outbreak of World War II, huge chunks of Africa still belonged to Portugal, Italy, Spain, Belgium, Britain, and France.

Yet there was a crucial distinction between British and American racism. Whereas British disparagement targeted mostly foreigners, the group pilloried by Americans lived within the nation's borders. What alarmed Ben Tillman was the multitude of blacks in his native state, not in Asia or Africa. " 'We've got 'em here,' " a white Texan in Johnson's 1912 novel, *The Autobiography of an Ex-Coloured Man*, protests to a Northern liberal,

and we've got 'em to live with, and it's a question of white man or nigger, no middle ground. You want us to treat niggers as equals. Do you want to see 'em sitting around in our parlors? Do you want to see a mulatto South? To bring it right home to you, would you let your daughter marry a nigger?[201]

The English were spared the specter of intimacy. Britain ruled over millions of black and brown human beings, but these inferior races huddled on distant continents, thousands of miles away. The nonwhite population of the kindgom itself, though greater than previously thought, was still tiny compared to that of the United States, where in states like Mississippi and South Carolina the turn-of-the-century proportion of blacks approached 60 percent. Racial trespass as a white nightmare simply did not have the same urgency for Britons as it did for Americans—and above all for Americans from south of the Mason-Dixon Line.

Few of whom could compete with Thomas Dixon in envisaging the horrors of black lawlessness. Or rather, what Dixon focused on was the menace of black physicality—dark and rank flesh obtruding itself into civic and social spaces where it had no right to impose and where, worst of all, it defiled pure white flesh with its adjacency. Dixon's racism was of the postbellum variety that abhorred nothing so much as the degradation of contact with negritude. His descriptions of black characters are obsessive in their iteration of bestiality and aberrance: Lydia Brown has "the fierce temper of a leopardess" (57);[202] Silas Lynch's yellow eyes and protruding brow are vestiges of "the primeval forest" (93); Gus's apelike head sits atop a squat neck suggestive of "the lower order of animals" (216); and Old Aleck's bulging stomach looks like "an elderly monkey's" (249). These characters carry with them the miasma of "African odour" (246). Whites in league with blacks contract the contagion of bodily deformity. Congressman Austin Stoneman, the Radical Republican villain based on Thaddeus Stevens, suffers from a club foot "resembling more closely an elephant's hoof" than a human appendage—and has the additional disfigurement of a hair piece "too small" for his massive forehead (39).

Dixon's blacks do not simply resemble animals; they literally *are* animals in that they inhabit the domain of the body. Activities of mind—spirituality, reflection, self-denial—are foreign to them. Their notion of love is rape. Educating them is impossible, because they lack the capacity for mental improvement.

Since the dawn of history the Negro has owned the Continent of Africa—rich beyond the dream of poet's fancy, . . . [Yet] he lived as an ox, content to graze for an hour. . . . He never sawed a foot of lumber, carved a block, or built a house save of broken sticks and mud. . . . [He] stole his food, worked his wife, sold his children, ate his brother, content to drink, sing, dance, and sport as the ape! (292)

Civilized life, to Dixon, involves the transcendence of animal appetite; negritude is its antithesis. Former slaves elected to the state legislature bawl, drink, and jostle in the hall of deliberation, "barbarism strangling civilization by brute force" (267). The aspiring black politicians of the occupied South have the skills of demagogic immediacy; they sway their auditors with gesture and oratorical emotionalism. Silas Lynch's voice "stirred a Negro audience as by magic" (93). Aleck "was a born African orator, descended from a long line of savage spell-binders, whose eloquence in the palaver houses of the jungle had made them native leaders" (249). Hypnotic performers on the Reconstruction stage, these men cannot rise to the level of rationality or culture; Aleck, not surprisingly, can neither read nor write. To send a black man to college, as Stoneman has done with Lynch, is to enlarge the scope of his lusts without in any way refining his character. Lynch's fondest hope, the goal to which he exhorts his followers, is to enter the former master's house and—once again, the endlessly repeated fantasy—marry the white man's daughter.

Homage to Southern landscape and climate, to the lush fertility of South Carolina, paradoxically complements revulsion from black physicality. Phil Stoneman professes to "love these green hills and mountains, these rivers musical with cascade and fall, these solemn forests." The South would be a garden paradise, he adds, were it not "for the Black Curse" (282). Barely removed from nature, blacks pollute the natural environment. The only way to purify the land is to empty it of them. Dixon heartily concurs with his imaginary Lincoln, whom he makes a fanatical advocate of colonization. The president tells an irate Austin Stoneman that he favors returning the former slaves to "the tropics" and erasing every trace of nonwhite personhood from the United States. "The Nation cannot now exist half white and half black, any more than it could exist half slave and half free" (46–47).

*The Clansman*'s vision of black animality descends directly from slavery. As is clear from abolitionist classics like the *Narrative of the Life of Frederick Douglass, an American Slave* (1845), Southern planters sought to confine their slaves to the level of nature and the body. Slaves were forbidden to read and write—in many states, it was illegal for their owners to teach them to do so—and they were kept in ignorance of the indices of human culture: their birthdates and the identity of their (often white) fathers. They might have been told that they were born in planting season or the fall, but they would "know as little of their ages as horses know of theirs." Douglass affirmed his right to culture against the dehumanization of enslavement by subtitling his autobiography, *Written by Himself*.[203]

In its suspicion of embodiment, its fear of black propinquity as contaminating, Dixon's novel dovetails with the modernist trend toward incorporeality. It has a not-so-secret sympathy for modes of cultural expression from which material being has been effaced, of which in 1905 the latest example was the cinema. The book calibrates whiteness with ideality and negritude with qualities operative on the stump and on the stage: powerful voice, speech, physical magnetism—in a word, the body. History, perversely, lent support to Dixon's dichotomies. The theater mounted a real event that had the effect, so Dixon believed, of wrongly advancing the black man. Hope for national reconciliation on terms favorable to the South was snuffed out in 1865 in a Washington playhouse. Book 1, chapter 6 of *The Clansman* is entitled "The Assassination." It relates how Lincoln, according to his fictional portrait a son of Kentucky and a friend of the defeated Confederacy, met his death at Ford's Theater while watching a performance of *Our American Cousin*. His killer was the actor, John Wilkes Booth.

While Dixon rewrote *The Clansman* as a play, the novel's longevity and influence stem from its adaptation for the screen. This pernicious saga found its true home in the silent ghostly pictures. Dixon appears to predict as much, or at least he intuits an antipathy between insubstantial images and the oppressively physical African. After Gus rapes Marion, the distraught girl and her mother leap to their deaths to escape the dishonor of black violation. The doctor who examines the corpses discovers an image of the rapist etched on the retina of the dead mother, and, armed with this "evidence," the Klan swings into action, summarily executing Gus and reasserting white rule over the South. (Dixon's baleful influence on the movies didn't end with *The Clansman*. Another of his fictions was adapted for the film *Bolshevism on Trial* [1919] and helped ignite the "Red scare" that followed the Russian Revolution.)

Out of the connections Dixon glimpsed, Griffith fashioned great cinema. In *The Birth of a Nation* he advances "A Plea for the Art of the Motion Picture" (in the wording of an introductory intertitle) as an elite cultural successor to "Shakespeare and the Bible" and as an adversary of the ignorant and grossly embodied black man. Griffith's movie is imperial on many levels. It can be viewed, most obviously, as an affirmation of reunited nationhood. The film also configures blacks as Indians, and the Klan as the U.S. Cavalry, in a deliberate invocation of Manifest Destiny, and it poses as the handmaiden of both secular and providential history. Further, *Birth* takes pains to distance itself from artisanal anonymity. It proclaims cinema's maturation as capitalist enterprise. Prominently displayed in the upper corners of every intertitle frame is the name, "Griffith," and at the bottom, center, appear the initials "DG," leaving no doubt as to the picture's ownership. (Copyright law had been amended to include the movies just three years earlier.)

But in nothing is Griffith's ambition more high-flown than in his idea of the motion pictures as the aesthetic vanguard of modernity. Narrative film, as epitomized by *Birth*, has evolved into a complex and denatured art rising superior to its disreputable origins in the nickelodeon. For the man who more than any other shaped the temporal and spatial syntax of the movies, the medium's purity—rather like that of his white heroes and heroines—consists in its distance from the products of miscegenated culture.

To Griffith, the movies are an all-encompassing form; they contain and surpass every rival discursive technology. *Birth* conscripts writing in its use of intertitles, including quotations from Woodrow Wilson and the Bible; history, in its reproduction of "Historical Facsimiles" based on photographs and in its staging of such national events as the South's victory at Bull Run and Sherman's torching of Atlanta; painting, in its careful composition of iconographic scenes like the celebrated shot of the battlefield dead titled "War's peace"; photography, not only in the examples cited above but in the miniature Ben Cameron carries of Elsie Stoneman, which comes to life, as it were, when the real Elsie nurses "the little Colonel" back to health after he is wounded in battle; and the drama, in its replaying of passages from the Ford's Theater production of *Our American Cousin* and in its implicit use of stagehands to provide continuity ("One Moment Please While We Change Reels"). *Birth* was also the first movie to have its own specially composed musical score.

Griffith appeals to literateness and the novel as the cinema's most pertinent models. *Birth's* grandiose comprehensiveness specifies its parentage in the imperial fictional genre of the nineteenth century and in the power to read and write that had certified antebellum whites as the superior race. The film begins with acts of literacy: the Stoneman brothers compose a letter for the Camerons, their old school chums from South Carolina, and then the camera jumps to the Cameron home in Piedmont, where the missive is received while the family patriarch pores over his newspaper. Plentiful captions, some padded with polysyllabic words, make demands upon the moviegoer's literacy. The requirement is not a trivial one in a nation of non-English-speaking immigrants and poorly educated blacks. (Even in a more racially and ethnically homogeneous society like Britain the use of the printed word in silent pictures could create difficulties for unlettered, working-class viewers.)[204] But the more important skill at "reading" is visual: the viewer has to make sense of Griffith's narrative techniques, whose complexity raises the cinema above mere entertainment or melodrama.

As Griffith's methods, particularly his use of parallel action or montage, have been extensively analyzed elsewhere,[205] it will be sufficient to note the intellectual challenge his film presents, the difficulty the uninitiated spectator experiences in following the narrative progression. (I have watched the video with a twelve-year-old, who lost interest after several minutes and complained, "How do you know what's going on?") Rapid intercutting among scenes causes vertiginous shifts in time and space, two or even three story lines unfold simultaneously, and disorienting accelerations in tempo, from virtual stasis to chaotic activity, buffet the viewer. These devices, as Sergei Eisenstein has emphasized, are patterned on the novel. Griffith, a fan of Dickens, took his cues about scenic transition from the greatest Victorian novelist.[206]

Dickens was a flamboyant melodramatist; his fictions, with their reliance on sentiment and their caricatured villains and heroes, suggest the popular theater rather than, say, the narratives of Theodore Dreiser or Gertrude Stein. To the present-day viewer, Griffith's film can also seem extremely stylized, more given to overstatement than to realism. Much, perhaps most, of the acting verges on bombast: exaggerated bodily poses combine with telegraphic facial grimaces to produce a style redolent of the stage and, by our lights, unsuitable for the movies. Unaided by speech, acting for the silent pictures is arguably an atavism compared to the "natural" method preferred by the late Victorian theater: it looks like a reversion to pantomime. And the stage as a structuring principle makes itself felt in *Birth* in various other ways too—in the grand sweeping staircase of the Cameron home, for example, which functions less as a lifelike setting than as an unchanging backdrop, or in the darkly encircled borders of the picture frame, which remind one of a furled curtain.

Yet there can be no doubt that Griffith aspired to something subtler and more inventive than is indicated by these residues of melodrama. If he poached on Dickens, he also had in mind the novel of his own day, a self-consciously modernist form with pretensions to the highest echelons of art. After all, this was a man (or rather "an artist") with epic dreams for his medium, a founding member of the piously named United Artists who had himself acted in plays by Oscar Wilde and Ibsen and who, even before he directed his first movie, liked to describe his profession as "writing." In an advertisement printed in the New York *Dramatic Mirror* six months before he began shooting *Birth* (and almost certainly written by himself), Griffith takes credit for "revolutionizing" the pictures and "founding the modern technique of the art." Among his contributions to elevating cinema "to the higher plane which has won for it recognition as a genuine art," he lists not only the "switchback" and "fade out" but also "restraint in expression."[207] However uneven in practice, this commitment to the sophisticated rendering of affect is meant to purge Griffith's film of theatrical excess and to send a message about its seriousness. Many of *Birth*'s best-known moments do in fact achieve a kind of brilliant understatement, as in the scene where Ben Cameron, having recovered from his wounds, returns to Piedmont and is drawn into the family home by his mother's arm.

Moreover, Griffith prizes verisimilitude in acting enough so that at times he risks confounding the moviegoer to obtain realistic results. A famous story about the making of *Birth* concerns Mae Marsh, the actress who plays the rape victim, "Little Sister." Griffith asked her if she had ever been truly terrified and how she had reacted to the experience, and Marsh is supposed to have replied, "I laughed." So he filmed the scene of the Union irregulars looting the Cameron mansion with the family cowering in the basement and Little Sister, against all commonsensical expectations, grinning and laughing hysterically.[208] It is an antisentimental sequence worthy of Henry James, dwarfing in psychological naturalism the predictable representations of emotion in popular theater and the nickelodeons.

These artistic "improvements" did in fact spell the end of the nickelodeon era and its residual ethos of audience participation. *Birth* was a cultural crossroads marking the definitive separation of the filmic narrative from the watching spectators. Griffith's historical spectacle affirmed the movies' position as legatee to the novel, conjurers of a sealed-off world on celluloid instead of in print. The *post-Victorian* novel, it should be emphasized—for the classical Hollywood style adumbrated in *Birth* was to forswear ruptures of diegetic integrity as surely as the realist novel renounced Dickensian apostrophes to the reader. *Birth* also laid claim to the "legitimate" theater's heritage. Its movement away from melodramatic stage conventions toward naturalistic autonomy was inseparable from Griffith's imposition of a $2 entrance fee, which priced the movies into middle-class respectability; from the March 1915 premiere at New York's fashionable Liberty Theater, where the film ran for an astonishing eleven months; and from the $100,000 Griffith spent to make the picture, which underlined its qualitative difference from the assembly-line "sausages" he used to grind out for Biograph, short, inexpensive features that might be compared to vaudeville skits or entr'actes. Griffith, as noted, had acted in dramas by Ibsen. His controversial masterpiece effected the triumphant transfer of Ibsenite realism from the theater to the screen.

Quite as important as an act of upgrading was Griffith's casting of well-known white performers as his major black characters. One hesitates to call this rooting out an "aesthetic" choice, although it may have seemed so to Griffith, because the use of actors in blackface shatters the supposed transparency of *Birth* even more flagrantly than do the pantomimic gestures.[209] But clearly Griffith wanted nothing to do with black physicality. (Or with pronounced physicality of any sort. He cast sylphic actresses [Lillian Gish, Mae Marsh] as his heroines, and he invented techniques like "hazy photography" to "erase imperfections" of the flesh. The quoted words are his.)[210] *Birth* neutralized the threat of miscegenation in the most literal way possible, through a stratagem that suggests nothing so much as the segregationist ruling of *Plessy v. Ferguson*: by eliminating nonwhite principals from the story.

Characters in blackface, it is true—as well as redface, yellowface, and brownface—had appeared in primitive pictures, including several of Griffith's own one-reelers for Biograph.[211] But African Americans had played roles too, and one of the most controversial films before *Birth*, the *Johnson-Jeffries Fight* of 1910, showed the first black heavyweight champion successfully defending his crown against a "great white hope." Once again, Griffith's epic announced a turning point, as it ossified the haphazard exclusions of its predecessors into a cultural decree. The virtual erasure of African Americans is part of the work's distancing from and domestication of nature. Griffith, who expressed bewilderment at charges of racism, intended both to soften *The Clansman*'s virulence and to banish what Dixon had called "the black abyss of animalism" (371). He dispensed with the consummated rape, not permitting Little Sister's body to be violated by Gus. (It is Gus who is the object of physical violence in the movie: Little Sister strikes him in her horror at his proposal of marriage, and he is later killed by the Klan, who fling his corpse onto Silas Lynch's porch.) Griffith finds the idea of interracial sex so monstrous that he adds a grisly touch not found in Dixon: near the end of the film, when the whites are beseiged in the cabin belonging to the Union veterans, Dr. Cameron holds a pistol to his unconscious daughter's head, ready to kill her lest she fall into the clutches of the black marauders.

Gus, Lynch, and Lydia Brown, the troika of black malefactors, are all played by whites in burnt cork and look less like African Americans than immigrants from Southern and Eastern Europe (by 1915 another object of nativist hysteria). A handful of nonwhite actors are scattered about the scene as extras, but none of them is granted entrance into the celestial city presided over by the Prince of Peace in the picture's final vision. The absence of blacks from the millennium, far from being an oversight, is the very condition that permits paradise to be regained: "the bringing of the African to America," explains an initial intertitle, poisoned the New World Eden by planting "the first seed of disunion." *Birth* admits animals into the frame, but only harmless ones: puppies, a dove, a squirrel. And the film's silence secures its audience from the profanation of jungle eloquence, anathematized by Dixon as the lethal corollary to black presence.

Griffith never lets us forget that the Klan is "a veritable empire." In this instance, he is quoting Wilson; the more familiar title of the organization, to which the movie also refers, is the "Invisible Empire." For the purposes of this essay, it would be hard to imagine a cognomen richer in implication. A few meanings suggested by the name would include: invisible understood as spiritual or godly, in contrast to the black (satanic, and all-too-visible) empire Silas Lynch plans to establish in the South. (In *The Clansman* Dixon makes Gus a budding demagogue and gives his full name as "Augustus Caesar," underlining the rapist's link to worldly, tyrannical power.) The film's fantasy of the New Jerusalem consolidates the millennial aspect of the Klan's title: a futuristic dominion of the light-skinned as the elect, as Christ's chosen people. (In the scriptures, the descent of the heavenly city is preceded by the "passing away" of the physical earth.) "Invisible Empire" further evokes the cinema itself, Griffith's medium of disincarnated signs, the referents of which are unseen. And, finally, the term "Invisible Empire" can be applied to twentieth-century American global mastery, an imperial regime without instantiation in colonial administrators and armies of occupation.

Dixon's brand of modernist disembodiment opened a gap between the movies and other forms of American entertainment. The breach was widest in popular or mass culture. *Birth* eschewed the black-white symbiosis that energized contemporaneous developments in music, dance, and literature. James Weldon Johnson, who achieved fame writing lyrics for Broadway musicals while Dixon was winning his director's spurs at Biograph (and who could never have worked in Hollywood himself), has described this intermingling in *The Autobiography of an Ex-Coloured Man*:

> Four things . . . demonstrate that they [black people] have . . . the power of creating that which can influence and appeal universally. The first two of these are the Uncle Remus stories, collected by Joel Chandler Harris, and the Jubilee songs, to which the Fisk singers made the public and the skilled musicians of both America and Europe listen. The other two are rag-time music and the cake-walk. No one who has travelled can question the world-conquering influence of rag-time. . . . In Paris they call it American music.[212]

Every one of the genres mentioned by Johnson is a demotic art that gained elite acceptance. Every one involves immediacy, although the Remus folktales, originally an oral phenomenon, were transcribed by a white man. To the list might be added jazz music. All the forms bring the white spectator into the presence of African-American performers. They are arts that encourage interaction and reciprocity. The post-Griffith scopic regime exorcised negritude and sociability from the film-going experience, recognizing—and recoiling from—the integrationist potential of the combination. For Griffith, the pruning away of blackness was the foundational event for both nation and cinematic culture, the necessary amputation that authorized the mainstream Hollywood style and the reunion of North and South. And "foundational event" is meant deliberately here. There was *no* true American nation, Griffith believed (and his title reminds us), until the Klan reconciled the sections by ostracizing racial otherness. *Birth*'s release was timed to coincide with the Golden Anniversary of the Civil War; like the election of a white Southerner to the presidency, the movie supposedly bound up the lingering wounds from the country's internecine bloodletting. (It should be recorded that Griffith's efforts at cinematic boosterism bore institutional fruit: in 1940, eight years before his death, his films were honored with a retrospective at the Museum of Modern Art.)

"My experience," said Booker T. Washington in 1901, in his actual autobiograpy of a postbellum "coloured man," *Up From Slavery*, is that there is something in human nature which always makes an individual recognize and reward merit, no matter under what colour of skin merit is found. I have found, too, that it is the visible, the tangible, that goes a long way in softening prejudices. The actual sight of a first-class house that a Negro has built is ten times more potent than pages of discussion about a house that he ought to build, or perhaps could build.[213]

*The Birth of a Nation* helped ensure that, for half a century, visible and tangible evidence of black ability would be largely excluded from the "world-conquering" American cinema.

In earlier sections of this essay, I have speculated on the associations between the movies and Turner's frontier thesis, both of them products of the 1890s. Another connection is suggested by Griffith's erasures. Turner's catalogue of climactic events—imperialism, the end of open space, corporate capitalism, and populist resistance—entails a significant omission: the harrying from public view of African Americans. The frontier postulate, with its unswerving focus on the line separating wilderness from civilization, represses the equally influential Mason-Dixon Line demarcating North from South.[214] A decade after Turner's speech, in *The Souls of Black Folk* (1903), W. E. B. Du Bois called attention to another, and related, line that the historian's argument overlooks. "The problem of the Twentieth Century," wrote Du Bois, "is the problem of the color-line." The frontier thesis gives scholarly legitimacy to the national amnesia about the former slaves. In partnership with the movies, it offers the consolations of displacement to a people weary of moral reproach, substituting infinite promise and national greatness for the torment of racial and sectional strife.

It would be unwarranted to conclude from this discussion that the cinema entrenched itself in the United States because it dematerialized or rendered undiscernible the large native minority population. By the same token, it would be absurd to claim that the theater felt at home in England because of the scarcity of nonwhite residents until after decolonization. And we should not ignore the fact that a subculture of "race movies," featuring minority performers and geared to minority audiences, existed in the ghettoes. Still, it seems likely that *some* bond exists between white American receptivity to the motion pictures, a medium of bodily effacement, and the pressure of living in proximity to millions of black people, who over the course of a century were made to disappear from sight. The self-proclaimed invisibility of the Klansmen ended up as the lot of their victims, the African-American community. (Ralph Ellison's *Invisible Man* [1952] is the canonical literary treatment of that condition.) At the very least, one would have to say that the mainstream cinema's doing away with (black) persons enhanced its standing in the United States. As for the English, they may have been less enthusiastic (and less resourceful) about exorcising the flesh-and-blood performer in part because they were so racially uniform a people. They didn't feel the same need to convert from stage to screen because there simply weren't that many black bodies around to desubstantialize.

American blacks were quick to sense the threat to their interests that *Birth* represented. They recognized in its ostracisms and caricatures a flagrant attempt to annul what little progress they had made since Emancipation. The film, said one critic, was "vicious, untrue, and unjust" and had been "produced to cause race friction." In the short run, events justified such fears: Griffith's picture succeeded in reviving the Klan, which had been moribund for thirty-five years. But *Birth* had benign (if unintended) consequences too. Its racism aroused African Americans to national collective protest for the first time in their history. "Organize! Organize! Organize!" cried the *Amsterdam News*, and black activists whipped up enough negative publicity to force cuts and delay openings in several cities.[215] The agitation gave an important stimulus to the embryonic NAACP and provided inspiration for the 1917 Silent Protest Parade against that summer's rash of lynchings. It opened the door for the campaign (led by James Weldon Johnson) to make lynching a federal crime. *Birth*, which did so much to set back race relations in America, awakened the indestructible will to rectify the damage. Another "birth" must thus be dated from the film's release in 1915: that of the civil rights movement and the struggle for black visibility.

## Sameness and Difference

Class served much the same function in Britain that race did in the United States. It established gradations of worth, marked out lines of inclusion and exclusion. And the theater worked to reinforce the principle of difference in English life. The expulsion of blacks from the cinematic "invisible empire" fed the illusion of consanguinity between the movie star and the viewer. To democratize the metaphor, the movies became a kind of "white republic" where all were equal. The indelibility of social division in England had the opposite effect. It fortified the impassable barrier between the classically trained stage performer and the popular audience.

Not that the British, even in the age before wholesale foreign immigration, were immune to racial or ethnic prejudice. Many took it for granted, as a popular joke had it, that "the niggers begin at Calais." But if the French were bad, the colored populations of the Empire were considerably worse. The humblest Briton rated higher on the scale of humanity than the most advanced native of Asia or Africa. In Paul Scott's *The Day of the Scorpion* (1968), a British officer of modest birth who is stationed in India, Ronald Merrick, reflects on his hobnobbing on equal terms "with people who would snub him at home." Neither talent nor his uniform is what has gained him acceptance, Merrick decides:

> What they had in common was the contempt they all felt for the native race of the country they ruled. He could be in a room with a senior English official and a senior Indian official and he could catch the eye of the English official who at home would never give him a second thought, and between them there'd be a flash of compulsive understanding that the Indian was inferior to both of them, as a man.

Dark-skinned persons who aped their betters, the colonials known as "WOGs" (Westernized Oriental Gentlemen), were held in special contempt as an affront to the natural order of things.[216]

Historians of British imperialism believe that this rigid demarcation between colonizer and aboriginal subject—what James Morris has termed "one standard for Britons, one for the rest"—was a relatively late development, a disillusioned reaction to the Indian Mutiny of 1857.[217] Whatever its provenance, the pattern of racial difference and identity, of discrimination from nonwhite natives and rough parity among white administrators, was nurtured by the physical closeness of occupation and inverts the American experience. In the case of the English, strict racial hierarchizing rooted itself in the colonies, where the indigenous peoples lived; and racial solidarity among the dominant group replaced the vigilant policing of class boundaries that defined daily existence in the metropole. Imperial racial categories were reconstituted in the homeland only belatedly, in response to increased migration, and did not stiffen into exclusionary policy until well into the twentieth century.[218]

But the English brand of transplanted egalitarianism had its limits. In the passage from *The Day of the Scorpion*, the bond of recognition between Merrick and his superior depends on the native official being literally present in the room. "And then if the Indian left the room the understanding would subtly change. He [Merrick] was then the inferior man."[219] So resilient are class feelings among his countrymen, according to Scott, that racial prerogative can suspend them only temporarily.

On the American side, something of a consensus has emerged that the subordination of blacks, first as slaves, then as racial inferiors, constructed whiteness as a privileged category, all of whose members were judged to be equal. (And this is not to mention the forced removal and near liquidation of indigenous Americans, actions that similarly strengthened ruling group identity through the effacement of otherness.) Equality is, of course, a foundational American principle, and racial injustice contradicts the democratic idea. But for much of the country's history, the contradiction has been more theoretical than actual. The white Southerners revolting against King George III simultaneously denied freedom to blacks; Thomas Jefferson, draftsman of the ringing declaration, "all men are created equal," was himself the owner of slaves. Even Walt Whitman, peerless as a singer of human equivalence, believed in white supremacy. The poet who penned the democratic epic, "Song of Myself" in 1855 ("I celebrate myself / And what I assume you shall assume, / For every atom belonging to me as good belongs to you"), was the same man who three years later asked the rhetorical question, "Is not America for the Whites?" and answered with the words, "And is it not better so?"[220]

One would not wish to overstate either the extent or the permanence of this racial dynamic. (Some would say that neither *can* be overstated.) While American egalitarianism has always rested on exclusions, it has also expanded over time to incorporate its erstwhile victims. Whitman's song of the protean self, or Emerson's "representative man," posit a democratic sameness, an infinite substitutability whereby every member of society can imagine changing places with every other member.[221] The English, with their firmer sense of class division, do not enjoy the same degree of imaginative latitude. And the movies might be seen as prototypically American not simply because of their collusion in the republic's problematic universalism but also because of the belatedness of their making room for the excluded.

American egalitarianism has been a constitutive element of the nation's "free-trade" empire. Whereas British territorial imperialism reinforced a conviction of difference from the subaltern, American absence or nonpossession has proven perfectly compatible with the ideology of sameness. From the Spanish-American War to liberate the Philippines from their European oppressors, through the idealism of Wilson's Fourteen Points, to the multinational corporations of today, Americans have wanted other peoples to be *like*, not disparate from, themselves. We have pressed foreigners to adopt our political system and free-market economy, and we have importuned them to buy our computers, our software, our airplanes, our graduate education, our clothes, our sneakers, our fast food, our popular music, our television programs, and our cinema. Their wish to imitate our movie and rock stars and to "be like" our sports heroes fills us with pride, not scorn for their social climbing.

The theater and the movies stake out antithetical positions on the values of difference and sameness, or of hierarchy and individual duplication. The drama's investment in the social distinction between superior and inferior has persisted most overtly in the scaling of seat prices, and in the spectator's closeness to or distance from the action. Seventeenth-century aristocrats would often sit on the stage as a token of their importance. Seating arrangements were formalized at public playhouses like London's Globe on a tripartite model, with the classes physically separated into gallery, pit, and high-priced boxes. The Victorian era refined, or rather simplified, these divisions. The better sort attended the legitimate theaters of the West End, while the working classes sought their entertainment in the music halls.

Theatergoing also entails a more covert kind of differentation or nonequivalence: the line separating the performer from the spectator. Hypothetically, it would be possible to trace this distinction to an ancient and ascriptive origin in the Renaissance. In the masques of the English court, the monarch and his retinue themselves donned costumes and played leading roles. Ben Jonson wrote a part for Queen Anne as Bel-Anna, Queen of the Ocean; Henry Prince of Wales was cast as Oberon; King James I as Neptune. Despite the lowly rank of public actors, performances by royalty in private settings were deemed acceptable, even exemplary. "A King," said James, "is as one set on a stage, whose smallest actions and gestures, all the people doe gazingly behold." The masques rehearsed the monarch's status as the cynosure of all attention, a royal actor before the kingdom. It has been suggested that these flattering court allegories functioned as a kind of idealized commonwealth in which kingly authority, under siege from the Puritans and other opponents of divine right, reigned supreme.[222]

Almost four centuries later, the figure on stage still inhabits a different order from the watching public. What creates the distinction in the present-day theater is talent and training, the qualities which have set the performer on a platform in the first place. English dramatic actors are masters of a repertory of "elocution, deportment, gesture, and countenance" (as William C. Macready put it in the mid-nineteenth century).[223] They tend to be extremely conscious of having acquired a classical technique which cannot be learned (by G. B. Shaw's count) "in three weeks, or even three years."[224] Study, repetition, and skill are necessary if one is convincingly to incarnate someone else.

John Gielgud, along with Olivier the premier English actor of the mid-twentieth century, claims that the secret of good acting consists in learning to overcome the self. Craft must replace (or at least supplement) the natural instinct to take one's graces and infirmities as the standard for others. Gielgud faults his youthful self for indulging in premature Method:

> I could not imagine a young man unless he was like myself. My own personality kept interfering. . . . In rehearsing Hamlet, I found it at first impossible to characterize. . . . All through rehearsals I was dismayed by my utter inability to forget myself while I was acting. It was not until I stood before an audience that I seemed to find the breadth and voice which enabled me suddenly to shake off my self-consciousness and live the part in my imagination, while I executed the technical difficulties with another part of my consciousness at the same time.

Peter Brook comments that for Gielgud the imitative faculty can never relax. It is an instrument that has to be honed ceaselessly: "the sifting, the weeding, the selecting, the dividing, the refining and the transmuting are activities that never end."[225]

The accomplished actor, in short, fits F. Scott Fitzgerald's definition of the very rich: different from you and me. (The difference, it should be emphasized, does not obstruct the momentary intimacy between actor and audience that is produced by the play. On the contrary, it makes that feeling of contact possible because it enables the actor to excel at the impersonation of character.) A Briton might object, and rightly so, that few of today's stage performers hail from the wealthy or patrician classes. They are far more likely to have worked their way up from common beginnings. But as their statements suggest, London's best actors are also people of rare natural endowment and professional expertise. Their success, like that of musicians or scientists from underprivileged backgrounds, testifies to the English readiness to recognize special talent whatever its source (a readiness that never quite annuls the stigma of class identity). The dramatic actor, while he or she may be an aristocrat of skill rather than of lineage, is a being apart, a person of indisputable artistic superiority who can act a lot better than the rest of us. The transparency of democratic selfhood stops at the theater door. A John Gielgud or a Vanessa Redgrave is not interchangeable with members of the public.

But a movie star often is. I have already touched on some of the ways that format and ideology collude to foster an idea of the film actor as untutored "being." Integral to this notion of selfhood is a supposition of leveling, of commonness and interchangeability. The movie actor, to be sure, seems more special than ordinary. But the specialness, as one critic has aptly observed, is "a blown-up version of the typical." *Anyone* can supposedly become a star, just as in theory any American can live out the dream of rags to riches. The much-publicized stories of actors being discovered on drugstore stools or while folding their wash in laundromats underscore the universality of the phenomenon, the myth that the most quotidian sort of person can achieve renown and fabulous wealth by simply being him- or herself. In this conception of democratic celebrity, the public is invited to bestow praise not because movie actors have painstakingly developed unique skills that differentiate them from us. They are praised because their singularity is a magnified image of our own. It is extremely difficult to impersonate another individual, as the stage performer strives to do. But it is a truism that anybody can play oneself. Nobody else can do it as well.[226]

This equivalence of actor and spectator is partly contrived, partly a function of medium and cultural values. From the early years of Hollywood to the present, from fan magazines like *Photoplay* (the first in the field, founded 1910) to late-night talk shows and MTV interviews, film stars—at the prompting of agents and PR people—have touted their typicality as a way of inviting the public to identify with them. They pass around snapshots of their children, tell stories about their pets, grouse about their diets. Their struggles, their likes and dislikes, are thoroughly recognizable.

Photography adds to the impression of one person's being comparable to another, perhaps because it is itself an agent of mechanical reproduction. Few people can ascend a stage and act, but it takes no skill to be photographed or filmed. Some of this interchangeablity, encouraged by the studios' wish to monopolize publicity, rubbed off on early movie actors. Most were identified not by name but by the roles they played: "the boy," "the girl with the ringlets," "an old man," "little sister." The generic bulked larger than the unique, and, though billing soon replaced anonymity, something of the primitive cinema's iterability has continued into the highly individuated star system of today.

The intuitive acting style theorized as the Method makes its subtext of egalitarianism or "Americanism" explicit. Viola Spolin, for one, dismisses the notion that the actor is a highly gifted individual who has mastered a demanding craft. "Everyone can act," she says. "Everyone can improvise. . . . We learn through experience and experiencing, and no one teaches anyone anything. . . . 'Talent' or 'lack of talent' has little to do with it." Julian Beck and Judith Malina go still further toward dispatching the bogeyman of special aptitude or superiority. They reject *any* division between the spectator and performer. Sounding like space-age Savonarolas (or, better yet, Rousseaus), the Becks admonish their disciples, "Don't imitate life. Live. Don't make graven images. Be."[227]

The Becks were founders of the Living Theatre, and their precepts are another reminder that in the United States the self-referential, antihierarchical mode of acting associated with the movie star has multiple sources in the culture—indeed, crops up in the very arena, the drama, colonized by the British. But in the province of art, it is above all the cinema that has actualized Whitman's injunction of democratic univeralism: *white supremacist* universalism, in the mainstream form confected by Griffith and perpetuated, until recently, by his Hollywood descendants.[228] Is it significant that even in this era of Spike Lee and Denzel Washington, of Whoopi Goldberg and Eddie Murphy, no black film actor has yet achieved box office parity with the top whites? Television has given us a Bill Cosby and an Oprah Winfrey, sports a Michael Jordan, but here again the motion pictures appear to have loitered behind in crossover stars. A hundred years after they ventured out of the nickelodeons, the movies still keep a certain aloofness from hybridized culture. Does *Birth* continue to cast its shadow over the medium?[229]

## Pros and Cons

Is today's fundamental opposition, then, between an impregnable and racially compromised cinema and a fraternal drama prophetic of restored cohesiveness? The benevolence of the anti-market-gospel/pro-live performance coalition shouldn't be exaggerated. English domesticating of epic theater has brought an increase in flexibility but also a narrowing of the Brechtian program. Brecht wanted to disconcert people and pique them into questioning the *doxa*; his end was revolution. The London theater, on the other hand, seems to have no political purpose at all—or perhaps no purpose other than to encourage self-congratulation on the part of a right-thinking minority, disdainful of mass culture and reveling in their insulation from the crudities of Hollywood.

Moreover, if the theater's mistrust of self-seeking individualism represents one side of its dissent from the American regimen, there may be other sides to that rejection which are considerably more problematic. Live entertainment's ceremony of fellowship conceals a host of contradictions. Despite efforts to broaden its base, the theater is still an elitist art attracting a well-to-do and mainly white clientele. Unlike the movies, and especially videos, even the subsidized stage charges prices out of the reach of most Britons. The community affirmed at the Barbican is highly restrictive, in terms both of race and class.

Historically, this exclusivity has been a defining attribute of English life, and a contrast to the United States. The legitimate English theater has always gloried in its unpopularity. Nineteenth-century advocates for a national playhouse identified the soundness of the project with its restrictions, stressing that much as the better sort represented the nation in Parliament (and served without pay until 1911), a national stage would be maintained by the imaginative few. The majority had neither the means nor the leisure to appreciate fine art, and proposals to lower prices were disapproved of on the grounds that such concessions would "cause the theatre to lose caste" (in the words of William Archer and Harley Granville-Barker's *Schemes and Estimates for a National Theatre* [1908]).[230] The association of the motion pictures with the American immigrant working class had its closest English parallel in the music halls; with the disappearance of the halls, the movies have joined the pubs and sports as the centers of nonelite recreation.

The English are a small, insular people who long resisted democracy and have never been receptive to the mass infusion of foreigners. Xenophobia (as revealed by daily news stories about the Common Market or British beef) is still rampant. Social hierarchy has always been taken for granted. An American learns with astonishment that, as late as 1948, businessmen could vote twice in parliamentary elections, once in their home constituencies and once where their businesses were located. (Graduates of Oxford and Cambridge enjoyed the same privilege, with the second vote in their university towns.)[231] British stratification, the firm sense of class roles and boundaries, might be considered, not as incompatible with cohesion, but as its necessary underpinning, as the glue that binds the national community together. Far from disseminating a spirit of democratic participation, then, the theater would be complicit in the entrenchment of the larger culture's social ghettoizing.

Interestingly, New Labour under Tony Blair, appalled by the growing separation between Britain's haves and have-nots, has assailed Thatcherite laissez-faire in the name of traditional community. Blair has revived the Disraeli slogan of England as "one nation," unified across class lines. He has invoked the very credo of social cooperation, long the property of Conservatives, that the Iron Lady spurned for entrepreneurial fundamentalism. Blair clearly means one nationism to stand for something more than either class struggle or aristocratic handout, but it remains to be seen whether this ideal, like the community of theatergoers at the subsidized playhouses, will simply reinscribe another set of exclusions. The idea's origin in quasi-feudal Tory paternalism doesn't promise well for egalitarian diversity.[232]

And what of the cinema? Does the medium's isomorphism with imperialist and corporate modernity tarnish it irreparably, consigning the viewer to a kind of passive submission before the display of privileged affect and mechanical wonders? I want to stress that this reading of America and the movies does *not* endorse the poststructuralist critique of film as replicating a regressive, infantalized subject who has lost all will to change the world.[233] My contention has been the far more historically anchored one that film, like a multiplicity of late nineteenth- and early twentieth-century social practices, reconfigures agency as deactualized and unapproachable. It marshals the imperialist design in the arena of culture by concentrating the power of decision-making into the hands of a few. Mainstream film, hailed as a millennial university of man, is a lecture, not a seminar; its structure of reception habituates the spectator to a sense of nonreciprocity.

But the spectator has the option of rejecting the message. Again, the argument is not that the screened image captivates and thus manipulates the moviegoer, who submits to its suggestions in a state of helpless stupor. The cinema alone simply doesn't exert that kind of totalizing influence over people's lives. It can operate as part of a general social disposition toward compliance, enforced by politics and economic insecurity, but even under those circumstances its effects are ambiguous, and anything but uniform.[234]

Something of film's ideological indeterminacy is suggested by the technologies that have converted the medium into a home-centered pastime. From one perspective, the VCR might be construed as a refutation of the cinema/theater dichotomy. Home video places an unprecedented degree of control in the viewer's hands. He or she can turn on the audiovisual entertainment at any time, interrupt it at random, and switch it off permanently if the movie is a disappointment. A new tape can be inserted, or half a dozen sampled before fixing on a final selection. The couch potato, equipped with a remote control, can impersonate a Brechtian director, replaying passages, constructing montage, freezing key moments in the picture. No theatergoer in London or New York enjoys so much choice, so many possibilities for intervention. Interactive "virtual reality" technologies still in the experimental stage may further expand the number of options. It may be possible to add and subtract characters from a film. The story line might be altered from tragedy to comedy, and a happy ending substituted for a sad one. Cinematic spectators disparaged for their quiescence before spectacle will metamorphose into lords of all they survey, able like Ariel to summon spirits at will and command them with a click of the remote.

New possibilities may filter into mainstream filmmaking from the bustling world of independent cinema. The appetite for product whetted by cable and video has translated into an upsurge of low-budget productions, some of which have managed to reach segments of the larger public. Sony Theaters, in partnership with Miramax, Fox Searchlight Pictures, Gramercy Pictures, and the Independent Film Channel, distributes a free brochure to patrons, titled *Independents*, which plugs documentaries, revivals, and foreign films, as well as relatively inexpensive features. A national magazine published in New York, *The Independent Film and Video Monthly*, keeps up with grassroots developments. Its pages are packed with reports on alternative filmmakers, festivals, art-houses, nonprofit venues, film schools, workshops, and seminars (almost all of them, be it noted, American).

So on the positive (if still imperial) side. But the same technologies multiplying viewer preference permit an altogether less sanguine inter-pretation. Home video's impression of choice may be the ultimate mys-tification of agency, the cunning capstone to a hundred years of filmic disempowerment. As viewers are showered with an ever greater variety of entertainment items, their possibilities for genuine input continue to shrink; they can can change the tape, but the production and ideological content of the art remain beyond their reach. (The "overstimulated sta-sis of too many choices and no chooser's manual," as David Foster Wallace has written of television.)[235] Indeed, fewer and fewer institu-tions are in a position *really* to control what happens on the screen, whether televisual or cinematic: to decide which movies get made and what kinds of subjects they address. The success of VCR technology has resulted in more, not less, media conglomeration, with a handful of international corporate giants—Time Warner, Disney/Capital Cities, Paramount Communications, MCA, and Rupert Murdoch's News Corporation, Ltd.—monopolizing popular cinematic production. Nor has there been a perceptible increase in product pluralism from the major players, as the blockbuster imperative has checked any urge to diversity. Hollywood studios are scrambling to copy *Independence Day*, not the far less lucrative Oscar-winner, *The English Patient* (1996) (which was promoted as having been financed and distributed by the "inde-pendent" Miramax, in reality a division of Disney).[236]

It may be pertinent, too, that the supposed enlargement of con-sumer choice has accompanied both the contraction of democratic par-ticipation, as voter turnout has plummeted to new lows, and an extraor-dinary redistribution of national wealth from the middle and working classes to the rich. Between 1977 and 1990, the share of wealth pos-sessed by the top 1 percent of American households doubled from 22 to a minimum of 44 percent, a level of inequality far surpassing anything in the socially stratified Old World.[237] In the same years, the VCR conquered living rooms across the country. Ordinary citizens were being flattened economically and watching their real choices drastically reduced. But they had the option of stopping *Forrest Gump* (1994) on the video so that they could send out for pizza and cokes.

This is no doubt to overrate the significance of a historical confluence. Moviegoing in the home and in the theater is never so resigned and impotent as detractors would have it. In the American case, one keeps coming back to the national bias toward independence, the habit, as Tocqueville put it, of carving out "a little circle of one's own." The spectator in his or her seat at the multiplex inhabits a space of private judgment, and it would be absurd to suppose that every viewer has the same reaction to, or arrives at the same conclusion about, a particular film.

Consider a story told by the African-American novelist James Baldwin. As a young child, Baldwin saw Bette Davis in the pictures—a woman, and a white woman at that—and realized that his frog-eyes, about which he had been cruelly teased, could be a weapon instead of a handicap. Film taught him a lesson indispensable to his development as an artist: he could thwart the world's intentions for him.[238] Many people have had a version of Baldwin's experience. And there is also the argument, shared by Walter Benjamin and the Founding Fathers, that the absence of aura or personal authority allows a greater degree of intellectual latitude, an enhanced capacity to challenge and reflect. It may be that even in its transparent realist style, the Hollywood cinema is more conducive to genuine democracy than the London stage. One need only add that democratic freedoms in the epicenter are in no sense incompatible with imperialism.

## Last Things, Strange Days

In Updike's *In the Beauty of the Lilies* the last scion of the Wilmot line, the cultist Clark, expires with a phrase from the movies on his lips, unable to distinguish between the thoughts framed by his brain and the words mouthed by apparitions on the white screen. Updike's theme of the inseparability of the real and the filmic has become a fascination of the movies themselves. The confusion takes a futuristic turn in *Strange Days* (1995), a thriller by the highly successful scriptwriter James Cameron, whose screenplay credits also include *The Terminator* (1984), *True Lies* (1994), and *Aliens* (1986). *Strange Days* is set in the final hours of December 1999, on the eve of the millennium. An ex-cop named Lenny Nero, played by Ralph Fiennes, traffics in the newest form of illicit entertainment. He is a drug dealer for a scopophilic culture, selling "SQUID" (Superconducting QUantum Interference Devices) tapes that record sensations directly from a person's cerebral cortex and that enable the buyer vicariously to enter another's experience. This isn't make-believe, Lenny assures a potential customer: "This is life. It's a piece of somebody's life."[239]

The gimmick has acquired a certain cachet in popular culture;[240] a second film, mislabeled *Unforgettable* (1996), also builds on the notion of reliving another's experience, although this time the other people are dead and a serum rather than technology is used for retrieving memories. The movies, inspired in their early days by the dream of "total reality," now self-reflexively contemplate the prospect of overcoming their sensory limitations—their deficiencies of taste, smell, touch, and so forth—and confronting the viewer with unmediated presence. In the future, the mechanical image will be "alive," and the distinction between theater and film, between flesh-and-blood actor and strip of celluloid, will disappear. Memory and dream, with which we began, will be at once cinematic and theatrical, because the movies, the stage, and our own inner lives will be impossible to tell apart.

## Afterword

> I was impressed . . . with the deference that the servants show to their "masters" and "mistresses,"—terms which I suppose would not be tolerated in America. The English servant expects, as a rule, to be nothing but a servant, and so he perfects himself in the art to a degree that no class of servants in America has yet reached. In our country the servant expects to become, in a few years, a "master" himself. Which system is preferable? I will not venture an answer.

The man who wrote these words, though himself American, was an Anglophile, and his inability to answer his question was genuine. He had an appreciation of rank. He deplored strikes, sought out and admired patrons, showed deference to the rich. A trip to England brought him gratifying recognition, and he reported that the British aristocracy, who were active philanthropists, commanded the love and respect of the masses. He returned home suspecting that a settled class system might have more to offer his people than the American free-for-all.

The author was the best-connected black man in the Jim Crow United States, Booker T. Washington.[241] English class society, as a network of mutual obligations, appealed to Washington because it seemed the antidote to American racism. Advancement may have been blocked for most, but Establishment Britons had a feeling of responsibility to the lower orders that Americans lacked, and this paternalism was reciprocated with affection from below. The nobility overlooked race to honor achievement. An American black who had made good had a better chance of being accepted by them than by the elite of his native land.

Washington of course has airbrushed the British. Less celebrated and well-off blacks were unwelcome, and acts of charity by titled rentiers did not extinguish class tensions. Distortions aside, however, an updated version of Washington's question hangs over this essay. To pose it as baldly as he did: Which is preferable, Britain and the ethics of the theater, or the United States and the cinematic vision? The fact that the question derives from Washington's helps to pinpoint the cruxes of the matter, which are race and class. (Gender, a major concern of both stage and film, does not offer anything like the same contrast in national experience.) The American movies have stood for egalitarianism but racial exclusion; the English theater has simulated a social harmony erected on stratification.

Like Washington, I have refrained from venturing a preference between these alternatives. Both seem to me at once admirable and indefensible. (I suspect that I have done a better job of conveying my skepticism about the movies than of stifling my [perhaps imaginary] nostalgia for community.) But the choice looks increasingly moot. Just as the theater and the pictures may be moving toward a kind of fungibility, so the differences between British and American society may be shrinking to the point where they are imperceptible. As any visitor to London can attest, English racial multiformity—as well as English racism—are noticeably on the rise. The ideal of cross-class responsibility is in decline. Tony Blair's first significant act upon taking office was to grant independence to the Bank of England, leaving it free to set short-term interest rates without worry about the impact on employment. His model, needless to say, was the Federal Reserve System. On the American side, as noted earlier, class inequalities have sharpened dramatically. In the 1920s, data on wealth concentration in Great Britain dwarfed the figures for this country, suggesting that America's reputation as a land of opportunity had some basis in fact. By the late 1980s, the trends had almost completely reversed, with wealth discrepancies easing in the United Kingdom and an entrenched upper class amassing the bulk of American assets. "Europe now appears the land of equality."[242]

This narrowing of national differences, if it continues, may have beneficial consequences for drama and film. The two media may be on the verge of a renaissance, not so much in their historic precincts as in the countries where, until now, they have operated as interlopers. TV ratings for the Tony Awards, hosted in 1997 by Rosie O'Donnell, have scored new highs. A $10 million fund has been proposed to subsidize serious dramas and inexpensive musicals on Broadway. In Great Britain, the film world is awash in excitement, giddy over the box office receipts for *Trainspotting* and the opening of new London studios. A scheme involving the National Lottery promises to pump more than a hundred million pounds into the domestic cinema. Let us hope that these praiseworthy cultural initiatives do not presage an Anglo-American monolith without the benefits of either egalitarian individualism or community and racial tolerance.

# Notes

1. See Jonas Barish, *The Antitheatrical Prejudice* (Berkeley and Los Angeles: University of California Press, 1981).

2. An important argument against the stage-to-movies transition is provided by Siegfried Kracauer, *Theory of Film: The Redemption of Physical Reality* (New York: Oxford University Press, 1960), 215–31. See also Leo Charney and Vanessa R. Schwartz, eds., *Cinema and the Invention of Modern Life* (Berkeley and Los Angeles: University of California Press, 1995). This collection of essays plays down film's theatrical and technological origins in favor of its relationship to phenomena like mail-order catalogs and window shopping.

3. Puttnam is quoted in Scott Lash and John Urry, *Economies of Signs and Space* (London: Sage, 1994), 128. Lash and Urry analyze the move to a "flexible accumulation" mode of film production (see 111–44 in particular).

4. British radio had a similar history. Lord Reith, first director-general of the BBC, spurned the U.S. model of commercial broadcasting for a "public service" mission. Reith's programming combined cultural instruction with antidemocratic imperiousness: "Few know what they want," he said of the public, "and very few what they need." Quoted in John Stevenson, *British Society, 1914–45* (London: Allen Lane, 1984), 410.

5. The quotation is from David Marc, *Demographic Vistas: Television in American Culture* (1984; rev. ed., Philadelphia: University of Pennsylvania Press, 1996), 188. Other useful studies of television include Todd Gitlin, ed., *Watching Television* (New York: Pantheon, 1986); Mark Crispin Miller, *Boxed-In: The Culture of TV* (Evanston, Ill.: Northwestern University Press, 1988); and Cecelia Tichi, *Electronic Hearth: Creating an American Television Culture* (New York: Oxford University Press, 1991).

6. Raymond Williams, *Television: Technology and Cultural Form* (1974; rpt., Hanover, N.H.: University Press of New England, 1992).

7. Mark Poster argues that computer writing instantiates deconstruction's destabilizing of logocentrism in *The Mode of Information: Poststructuralism and Social Context* (Chicago: University of Chicago Press, 1990), 99–128.

8. Perry Anderson, *English Questions* (London: Verso, 1992), 10.

9. Diana Rigg is quoted in the *Evening Standard*'s "1995 Theatre Guide."

10. John Heilpern, "Empire of the Stage," *Vanity Fair* (November 1995), 188–225.

11. A second visit to the King's Head, a year later during the peak tourist month of August, revealed some cosmetic changes but more crucial continuities. The play this time was *Emma*, an adaptation of the Jane Austen novel by Michael Fry. In its choice of trendy subject, as in much else, the King's Head had grown in ambition and commercial viability. A glossy playbill, complete with pink lettering and black-and-white photographs, announced the professional face-lift. The playbill featured a précis of the theater's history, a collection of blurbs (one from Tom Stoppard), and a list of "Notable and Award Winning" productions. Large contributions were invited from supporters (in exchange for such "plums" as having one's name immortalized on a bronze plaque), and an advertisement from the manufacturing firm of Farrow and Ball, which had donated "25 litres of paint for the set," appeared on the back cover.

The interior showed similar improvements (beyond the freshly painted set). There were real velvet theater seats in rows along the tables, which had been covered with blue checkered cloths. Antique stage lamps hung from the ceiling. And whereas on our previous trip the theater had been half empty, now the place was packed. Despite arriving in good time to collect our tickets, we had to join a long line and ended up sitting on a narrow bench at the back of the room.

But the informality and interaction so evident when we saw *The Secret Garden* were still on exhibit. The overcast London morning had darkened into a gloomy, blustery day. Throughout the performance, rain drummed on the roof, at times making it almost impossible to hear the actors. Water dripped onto the stage from a hole overhead. The five performers were too few for the necessary parts and, except for the actress playing Emma (Clara Salaman), were obliged to assume more than a single role. Jonathan Chesterman, who doubled—or rather tripled—as William, Mr. Elton, and Frank Churchill, kept getting wet and finally broke the tension with an improvised joke about the leak. The production concluded much as *The Secret Garden* had, with ushers asking patrons as they filed out to contribute their spare change to the King's Head building fund.

12. According to Penny Summerfield, a song written in 1877 by G. W. Hunt, "By Jingo," put the word into circulation. See Summerfield's essay, "Patriotism and Empire: Music-Hall Entertainment, 1870–1914," in John M. MacKenzie, ed., *Imperialism and Popular Culture* (Manchester: Manchester University Press, 1986), 25.

13. See Vachel Lindsay, *The Art of the Moving Picture* (New York: MacMillan, 1915), 200, 207–16, 287–89.

14. Lindsay, *Art of the Moving Picture*, 165, 151–70.

15. Benjamin discusses Poe in "On Some Motifs in Baudelaire," which appears in his *Illuminations*, ed. with an introduction by Hannah Arendt, trans.

Harry Zohn (New York: Schocken, 1969), 170–76.

16. For a vivid account of the railroad and modern industrialized consciousness, see Wolfgang Schivelbusch, *The Railway Journey: The Industrialization of Time and Space in the Nineteenth Century* (1977; rpt., Berkeley and Los Angeles: University of California Press, 1986), esp. chapter 4, "Panoramic Travel," 52–69. The detail about early theaters is in Tom Gunning, "The Cinema of Attraction: Early Film, Its Spectator and the Avant-Garde," *Wide Angle* 8, nos. 3–4 (1986): 65. Also relevant is Lynne Kirby's *Parallel Tracks: The Railroad and Silent Cinema* (Durham, N.C.: Duke University Press, 1997). Kirby calls the train "a mechanical double" for the movies (2).

17. The case for Los Angeles's supermodernity has been made by Mike Davis, *City of Quartz: Excavating the Future in Los Angeles* (New York: Verso, 1990).

18. There are many treatments of time in the movies. A good example is Jean-Claude Carrière, *The Secret Language of Film*, trans. Jeremy Leggatt (New York: Pantheon, 1994), 105–46. On time and the actor, see Debra Fried, "Hollywood Convention and Film Adaptation," *Theatre Journal* 39 (October 1987): 294–306. Steven Kern examines cinema as one of a host of late-nineteenth-century constructions—others include the X-ray, the telephone, Cubism, the theory of relativity, etc.—that led to new ways of conceptualizing time and space; see *The Culture of Time and Space, 1880–1918* (Cambridge: Harvard University Press, 1983).

19. Lindsay, *Art of the Moving Picture*, 191.

20. On some of the points in this paragraph, see also Gilbert Seldes, *The Movies Come from America* (New York: Scribner, 1937).

21. To be fair to Benjamin, his dialectical method does show a consciousness of space. Susan Buck-Morss elaborates on this aspect of his work in *The Dialectics of Seeing: Walter Benjamin and the Arcades Project* (Cambridge: MIT Press, 1991).

22. See Turner, "Contributions of the West to American Democracy" (1903), reprinted in *Frontier and Section: Selected Essays of Frederick Jackson Turner*, ed. Ray Allen Billington (Englewood Cliffs, N.J.: Prentice-Hall, 1961), 77–97.

23. Ibid., 90.

24. For material in this and the previous paragraph, see Chandler's magisterial *Scale and Scope: The Dynamics of Industrial Capitalism* (Cambridge: Harvard University Press, 1990). Chandler's work compares industrial firms in the United States, Great Britain, and Germany. Also relevant is Martin J. Sklar, *The Corporate Reconstruction of American Capitalism, 1890–1916: The Market, the Law, and Politics* (New York: Cambridge University Press, 1988). The figures on U.S. Steel are from Nell Irvin Painter, *Standing at Armageddon: The United States, 1877–1919* (New York: Norton, 1987), 179.

25. The characterization "pre-industrial" comes from Anderson, *English*

Questions, 139.

26. Chandler, *Scale and Scope*, 51–52, 244, 256.

27. Ibid., 292, 390–92.

28. The formulation is Martin J. Wiener's in *English Culture and the Decline of the Industrial Spirit, 1850–1980* (New York: Cambridge University Press, 1981), 6–7, passim. Wiener gets his account of the American viewpoint from Leo Marx's classic study, *The Machine in the Garden: Technology and the Pastoral Ideal in America* (New York: Oxford University Press, 1964). My next paragraph also draws upon Wiener. Wiener's thesis has been controversial, but it finds support in the work of Chandler, Anderson (especially his essay, "The Figures of Descent," in *English Questions*, 121–92), and P. J. Cain and A. G. Hopkins, "Gentlemanly Capitalism and British Expansion Overseas I: The Old Colonial System, 1688–1850," *Economic History Review* 49 (1986): 501–25, and "Gentlemanly Capitalism and British Expansion Overseas II: New Imperialism, 1850–1945," *Economic History Review* 50 (1987): 1–26.

29. I am quoting Cain and Hopkins, "Gentlemanly Capitalism and British Expansion Overseas I," 507.

30. On Thatcher's attempt to revive English competitiveness, see Charles Delheim, *The Disenchanted Isle: Mrs. Thatcher's Capitalist Revolution* (New York: Norton, 1995). Timothy Kidd fulminates against the London theater's supposed welfarism in "Between Revolt and Rancour: On Contemporary British Drama," *Encounter* 70 (January 1988): 62–68.

31. Roosevelt is quoted in Sklar, *Corporate Reconstruction of American Capitalism*, 78.

32. Still powerful as an indictment of the Populist mind is Richard Hofstadter, *The Age of Reform* (New York: Vintage, 1955). Lawrence Goodwyn argues for a more favorable view in *The Populist Moment: A Short History of the Agrarian Movement in America* (New York: Oxford University Press, 1978). A balanced assessment is scattered throughout Alan Trachtenberg, *The Incorporation of America: Culture and Society in the Gilded Age* (New York: Hill and Wang, 1982).

33. See Janet Staiger, "Dividing Labor from Production Control: Thomas Ince and the Rise of the Studio System," in Gorham Kindem, ed., *The American Movie Industry: The Business of Motion Pictures* (Cardondale: Southern Illinois University Press, 1982), 94–103; and David Bordwell, Janet Staiger, and Kristin Thompson, *The Classical Hollywood Cinema: Film Style and Mode of Production to 1960* (London: Routledge and Kegan Paul, 1985), 132–37. The quotation appears in *The Classical Hollywood Cinema*, 136.

34. See the prospectus by Halsey, Stuart & Co., "The Motion Picture Industry as a Basis for Bond Financing" (1927), in Tino Balio, ed., *The American Film Industry* (Madison: University of Wisconsin Press, 1976), 171–91. Simon N. Whitney discusses the divestment decree in "Antitrust Politics and the Motion

Picture Industry," in Kindem, ed., *The American Movie Industry*, 161–204.

35. Gore Vidal, *Palimpsest: A Memoir* (London: André Deutsch, 1995), 274.

36. John Gregory Dunne, *Monster: Living Off the Big Screen* (New York: Random House, 1997), 82–83, 143–82 (quotation from 83).

37. See Vincent Porter, *On Cinema* (London: Pluto, 1985), 63–65.

38. Painter, *Standing at Armageddon*, 38.

39. Miller's discussion of "The American Theater" (1955) appears in Robert A. Martin and Steven R. Centola, eds., *The Theater Essays of Arthur Miller* (New York: Da Capo Press, rev. ed., 1996), 31–50. Miller idealizes his medium here. For the actor, at least, the stage can involve a lot of tedious repetition. Not much freshness can survive five hundred or a thousand performances of the same play.

40. See John Kenneth Galbraith, *Money: Whence It Came, Where It Went* (1975; rev. ed., Boston: Houghton Mifflin, 1995), 26–57. My discussion of monetary policy relies on Galbraith and the following books: Marcello de Cecco, *The International Gold Standard: Money and Empire* (1971; 2d ed., London: Francis Pinter, 1984); Ronald L. McKinnon, *Money in International Exchange: The Convertible Currency System* (New York: Oxford University Press, 1979); and Lawrence H. Officer, *Between the Dollar-Sterling Gold Points: Exchange Rates, Parity, and Market Behavior* (Cambridge: Cambridge University Press, 1996).

41. Karl Polanyi, *The Great Transformation: The Political and Economic Origins of Our Time* (1944; rpt., Boston: Beacon Press, 1957), 192–200.

42. Galbraith, *Money*, 60.

43. Technically, the Bretton Woods Conference established a system of fixed exchange rates keyed to the dollar, which was itself convertible into gold (by foreigners only) at $35 an ounce. Eventually there was a drain on U.S. gold reserves, and President Nixon elected to rescind the equivalency measure. Edward M. Bernstein, a participant at Bretton Woods, refers to the Nixonian "abandonment of the anomaly of the convertibility of the dollar into gold when the United States was not on the gold standard." Quoted in Stanley W. Black, *A Levite Among the Priests: Edward M. Bernstein and the Origins of the Bretton Woods System* (Boulder, Colo.: Westview, 1991), 108.

44. For a scathing critique of British currency policy, see Edward Luttwak, "Central Banking: A New Religion," *London Review of Books* 18 (November 14, 1996): 3, 6–7.

45. I first encountered Ostrer's name in Michael Chanan, "The Emergence of an Industry," in James Curran and Vincent Porter, eds., *British Cinema History* (Totowa, N.J.: Barnes and Noble, 1983), 57–58.

46. Isidore Ostrer, *The Conquest of Gold* (London: Jonathan Cape, 1932). On "Alphas," see esp. chapter 8, "Ostrer's Paper Standard," 95–100.

47. This according to an article by Bernard Weinraub in the *New York Times*, March 5, 1997, D8.

48. Douglas Collins, *The Story of Kodak* (New York: Harry N. Abrams, 1990), 136.

49. A classic and still valuable study of American abundance is David M. Potter, *People of Plenty: Economic Abundance and American Character* (Chicago: University of Chicago Press, 1954).

50. The American journalist Bill Bryson, who has made a career of dissecting British mores, describes the temperamental differences in an amusing passage worth quoting at length:

> The British are so easy to please. It is the most extraordinary thing. They actually like their pleasures small. That is why, I suppose, so many of their treats—teacakes, scones, crumpets, rock cakes, rich tea biscuits, fruit Shrewsburys—are so cautiously flavourful. . . . Offer them something genuinely tempting—a slice of gateau or a choice of chocolates from a box—and they will nearly always hesitate and begin to worry that it's unwarranted and excessive, as if any pleasure beyond a very modest threshold is vaguely unseemly.
> "Oh, I shouldn't really," they say.
> "Oh, go on," you prod encouragingly. . . .
> All this is completely alien to the American mind. To an American the whole purpose of living, the one constant confirmation of continued existence, is to cram as much sensual pleasure as possible into one's mouth more or less continuously. Gratification, instant and lavish, is a birthright. You might as well say, "Oh, I shouldn't really," if someone tells you to take a deep breath.

See Bryson, *Notes from a Small Island* (1995; rpt., London: Black Swan, 1996), 98–99.

51. For the information in this paragraph, see Porter, *On Cinema*, 46–49; Collins, *Story of Kodak*, 24–27, 136–79; and Halsey, Stuart & Co., "The Motion Picture Industry as a Basis for Bond Financing," in Balio, *The American Film Industry*, 173.

52. Several British auteurs, notably Mike Leigh, have recently adopted a more improvisational style while still making what are by Hollywood standards exceedingly frugal movies. Leigh, who began his career as a playwright, is best known in the United States for *Naked* (1993) and *Secrets and Lies* (1996).

53. Alexis de Tocqueville, *Democracy in America* 2:104, trans. Phillips Bradley (1835; rpt., New York: Vintage, 1945).

54. Raymonde Carroll, *Cultural Misunderstandings: The French-American Experience*, trans. Carol Volk (Chicago: University of Chicago Press, 1988), 145.

55. Tocqueville, *Democracy in America* 2:114–17 (quotations from 114 and, on solitude, 106).

56. Lindsay, *Art of the Moving Picture*, 48–49, 39, 207, 163–64. Rousseau's diatribe against the drama appears in "Letter to M. D'Alembert on the Theatre" (1758), which is available in Rousseau, *Politics and the Arts*, trans. Allan Bloom (Ithaca: Cornell University Press, 1968).

57. Warren and Brandeis, "The Right to Privacy," *Harvard Law Review* 4 (December 1890): 193–220 (quotations from 195–96, 205).

58. The phrase is from "The Right to Privacy," 195.

59. For comparison of American and English privacy law, see Raymond Wacks, *Personal Information: Privacy and the Law* (Oxford: Oxford University Press, 1989), esp. 31–49; and Morris L. Ernst and Alan U. Schwartz, *Privacy: The Right to Be Let Alone* (1962; rpt., London: MacGibbon and Kee, 1968).

60. Porter, *On Cinema*, 102–107.

61. See Wolfgang Schivelbusch, *Disenchanted Night: The Industrialization of Light in the Nineteenth Century*, trans. Angela Davies (Berkeley and Los Angeles: University of California Press, 1988), 51–52.

62. For material on Disney and the theme parks, I have used Alan Bryman, *Disney and His Worlds* (London: Routledge, 1995).

63. The quote is from an official guide to Disney World (in Bryman, *Disney and His Worlds*, 73).

64. My sources for Stratford-upon-Avon are Norah Baldwin Martin, *Shakespeareland: Our Beautiful Homeland* (London: Blackie, n.d.); Levi Fox, *The Borough Town of Stratford-upon-Avon* (Norwich, Eng.: Corporation of Stratford-upon-Avon, 1953); and, particularly for the current scene, Robert Andrews et al., *Britain: The Rough Guide* (London: Rough Guides, 1996), 363–67.

65. See Gabler's *An Empire of Their Own: How the Jews Invented Hollywood* (New York: Anchor, 1988).

66. Gabler, *An Empire of Their Own*, 102, 79, passim.

67. See David Feldman, *Englishmen and Jews: Social Relations and Political Culture, 1840–1914* (New Haven: Yale University Press, 1994), 1–3. Disraeli's conversion did not spare him from virulent anti-Semitism during his political career. See Anthony S. Wohl's article, " 'Dizzi-Ben-Dizzi': Disraeli as Alien," *Journal of British Studies* 34 (July 1995): 375–411.

68. Feldman, *Englishmen and Jews*, 141–290; see also Eric Hobsbawm, *The Age of Empire: 1875–1914* (1987; rpt., New York: Vintage, 1989), esp. 40.

69. See John Berger, *Ways of Seeing* (Harmondsworth, Middlesex, Eng.: Penguin, 1972).

70. See Rudolf Arnheim, *Film as Art* (Berkeley and Los Angeles: University of California Press, 1957), 83–87; and André Bazin, *What Is Cinema?* 1:102–107, trans. Hugh Gray (Berkeley and Los Angeles: University of California Press, 1967).

71. Lindsay, *Art of the Moving Picture*, 259.

72. See Benjamin's "A Small History of Photography" in his *One-Way*

*Street and Other Writings*, trans. Edmund Jephcott and Kingsley Shorter (London: Verso, 1985), 240–57. Roland Barthes has described the photo as "the return of the dead" in *Camera Lucida: Reflections on Photography*, trans. Richard Howard (New York: Hill and Wang, 1981), 9. An excellent treatment of this subject is Martin Jay, *Downcast Eyes: The Denigration of Vision in Twentieth-Century French Thought* (Berkeley and Los Angeles: University of California Press, 1993), 435–93 ("The Camera as Memento Mori").

73. Douglas Gomery speaks of the "almost squalid viewing conditions of the multiplexes" in his article, "If You've Seen One, You've Seen the Mall," in Mark Crispin Miller, ed., *Seeing Through Movies* (New York: Pantheon, 1990), 49–80 (quotation from 71).

74. See Margaret R. Miles, *Seeing and Believing: Religion and Values in the Movies* (Boston: Beacon Press, 1996), 25–28.

75. Arthur Marwick, *British Society Since 1945* (London: Penguin, 1982), 101.

76. Tocqueville, *Democracy in America* 2:142–43.

77. On the British system, see Dennis Kavanagh, *British Politics: Continuities and Change*, 2d ed. (Oxford: Oxford University Press, 1990), quotation from 137; and Samuel H. Beer, *The British Political System* (1958; rpt., New York: Random House, 1974). Still invaluable is Walter Bagehot, *The English Constitution* (1864; rpt., London: Kegan Paul, Trench, Trubner, 1922).

78. Bagehot, *The English Constitution*, 227; see also Kavanagh, *British Politics*, 119.

79. Kavanagh, *British Politics*, 70.

80. Bagehot, *The English Constitution*, lxxiv, 21; for party discipline, see Beer, *The British Political System*, 33–36, on the "rule of collective responsibility."

81. Blair, as prime minister, has more latitude to operate than Clinton, who presides over a divided government, but in order to attain his position, the Labour leader had to reshape, not transcend, his party; he couldn't have been elected without Labour support in Commons.

82. See Hobsbawm, *The Age of Empire*, 84–111, 219–42, on the democratization of politics and the arts. Pierre Renoir (the Impressionist painter and father of Jean) is quoted in Louis Giannetti and Scott Eyman, *Flashback: A Brief History of Film*, 3d ed. (Englewood Cliffs, N.J.: Prentice-Hall, 1996), 138. Many people have championed the movies as a democratic medium; an interesting example (in view of the authorship) is Foster Rhea Dulles, "The Role of Moving Pictures," in Arthur F. McClure, ed., *The Movies: An American Idiom—Readings in the Social History of the American Motion Picture* (Rutherford, N.J.: Fairleigh Dickinson University Press, 1971), 21–39.

83. Frank Harris, quoted in Harold Perkin, *The Rise of Professional Society: England since 1880* (New York: Routledge, 1989), 62.

84. Fredric March, quoted in Kracauer, *Theory of Film*, 94.

85. Fonda is quoted in Louis Giannetti, *Understanding Movies*, 7th ed.

(Englewood Cliffs, N.J.: Prentice-Hall, 1996), 247. Giannetti's whole chapter on "Acting" (235–80) is helpful.

86. See Bordman, Staiger, and Thompson, *The Classical Hollywood Cinema*, 188–92, 362. The quotation, which is from one H. F. Hoffman and is dated 1912, appears on pp. 191–92.

87. See Giannetti, *Understanding Movies*, 249–63 (on stars) and 268–70 (on Method acting). On the greater "presence" of the movie actor, see especially Leo Braudy, "Acting: Stage vs. Screen," in Braudy's *The World in a Frame* (1976; rpt., Chicago: University of Chicago Press, 1984), 191–201.

88. See Debra Fried, "Hollywood Convention and Film Adaptation."

89. James Naremore questions the improvisatory quality of Brando's actions in *Acting in the Cinema* (Berkeley and Los Angeles: University of California Press, 1988), 193–212.

90. Marwick, *British Society Since 1945*, 214–17.

91. See ibid., esp. 206–208, 211–13. An exhaustive study of class markers, focusing on the French but still relevant, is Pierre Bourdieu, *Distinction: A Social Critique of the Judgement of Taste*, trans. Richard Nice (Cambridge: Harvard University Press, 1984).

92. Nancy Mitford, ed., *Noblesse Oblige: An Inquiry into the Identifiable Characteristics of the English Aristocracy* (1956; rpt., Westport, Conn.: Greenwood Press, 1974). The Waugh quote is from p. 93.

93. See Perkin, *The Rise of Professional Society*. But even Perkin concedes that England has "a reputation for being the most class-conscious nation in the world" (456).

94. Marwick, *British Society Since 1945*, 209, 218–19 (quotation from 218).

95. See the well-known essay by Warren I. Susman, " 'Personality' and the Making of Twentieth-Century Culture," in John Higham and Paul K. Conkin, eds., *New Directions in American Intellectual History* (Baltimore: Johns Hopkins University Press, 1979), 212–26. Fairbanks is described on p. 223.

96. The interview, which was conducted by Kenneth Tynan, appears as "The Art of Persuasion" in Toby Cole and Helen Krich Chinoy, eds., *Actors on Acting* (New York: Crown, 1970), 410–17 (the quotes are from 410–11).

97. John Wayne provides what is perhaps the most egregious example of this dissonance between a movie star's image and what he or she can really do. Wayne became a popular emblem of American (Cold) warriorhood, an identification he encouraged by producing and starring in hawkish films like *The Green Berets* (1968). Yet Wayne, a rabid patriot, had never served in the military. During World War II he chose advancing his career in Hollywood over fighting the Nazis. Garry Wills labels Wayne a "warless 'war hero' " in *John Wayne's America: The Politics of Celebrity* (New York: Simon and Schuster, 1997), 113, 156.

98. See Richard Slotkin, *Gunfighter Nation: The Myth of the Frontier in Twentieth-Century America* (New York: HarperPerennial, 1993), 237–52 (Wilson

cited on 240). The Wilson quote, though widely disseminated, may be apoc-
ryphal.

99. On opposition to the cinema, see Robert Sklar, *Movie-Made America: A Cultural History of American Movies* (New York: Vintage, 1976), 3–31; and Garth Jowett, *Film: The Democratic Art* (Boston: Focal Press, 1976), 74–89. Jowett cites Addams's reaction on pp. 78–79.

100. Lindsay, *Art of the Moving Picture*, 5.

101. Tom Gunning is informative on anonymity; see *D. W. Griffith and the Origins of American Narrative Film: The Early Years at Biograph* (Urbana: University of Illinois Press, 1991), 218–19.

102. See Lizabeth Cohen, *Making a New Deal: Industrial Workers in Chicago, 1919–1939* (New York: Cambridge University Press, 1990), 99–158.

103. The resemblance of movie viewing in the home to the nickelodeons has often been noted. See, for example, Bruce A. Austin, "Home Video: The Second-Run 'Theater' of the 1990s," in Tino Balio, ed., *Hollywood in the Age of Television* (Boston: Unwin Hyman, 1990), 319–49.

104. On Griffith and Dwan, see Scott Simmon, *The Films of D. W. Griffith* (Cambridge: Cambridge University Press, 1993), 1–2; on copyright, see Robert Sklar, *Movie-Made America*, 22; on the primitive cinema generally, see Charles Musser, *The Emergence of Cinema: The American Screen to 1907* (New York: Scribner, 1990).

105. The figure comes from Austin, "Home Video," 334.

106. Williams uses the phrase in speaking of television; see *Television: Technology and Cultural Form*, 20. The formulation has been picked up and revised in interesting ways by Anne Friedberg in her *Window Shopping: Cinema and the Postmodern* (Berkeley and Los Angeles: University of California Press, 1994). Friedberg associates postmodernism with "the commodification of a mobile and virtual gaze," xii.

107. I get this fact (and more) from the most comprehensive bibliographic compilation on the subject, Anthony Slide's *The Hollywood Novel: A Critical Guide to Over 1,200 Works* (Jefferson, N.C.: McFarland, 1995).

108. Studies of theater in the English novel abound. Good examples are Nina Auerbach, *Private Theatricals: The Lives of the Victorians* (Cambridge: Harvard University Press, 1990); Joseph Litvak, *Caught in the Act: Theatricality in the Nineteenth-Century English Novel* (Berkeley and Los Angeles: University of California Press, 1992); and on the eighteenth century, Susan Staves, "Fatal Marriages? Restoration Plays Embedded in Eighteenth-Century Novels," in Douglas Lane Patey and Timothy Keegan, eds., *Augustan Studies: Essays Presented to Irvin Ehrenpreis* (Newark: University of Delaware Press, 1985), 95–107.

109. On James and Howells as playwrights, see Brenda Murphy, *American Realism and American Drama, 1880–1940* (Cambridge: Cambridge University

Press, 1987).

110. John Updike, *In the Beauty of the Lilies* (New York: Knopf, 1996), 105.

111. Updike, *In the Beauty of the Lilies*, 436, 486.

112. Penelope Fitzgerald, *At Freddie's* (1982; rpt., London: Flamingo, 1989), 35.

113. Fitzgerald, *At Freddie's*, 74, 133.

114. Ibid., 56, 157.

115. Stanley Cavell, *The World Viewed: Reflections on the Ontology of Film*, enlarged ed. (Cambridge: Harvard University Press, 1979), viii–xxv, esp. ix and xx.

116. Gore Vidal, *Screening History* (Cambridge: Harvard University Press, 1992), 5.

117. See Sontag's essay, "Film and Theater" (1966), which has been reprinted in Gerald Mast, Marshall Cohen, and Leo Braudy, eds., *Film Theory and Criticism: Introductory Readings*, 4th ed. (New York: Oxford University Press, 1992), 362–74 (quotation from 370).

118. The "remake-revival" terminology is noted by Leo Braudy, although he construes its meaning differently (see *The World in a Frame*, 194–95).

119. See *The Autobiography of Benjamin Franklin*, ed. Leonard W. Labaree et al. (New Haven: Yale University Press, 1964), 62.

120. See Bagehot, *The English Constitution*, 8, 57, and generally, 33–88.

121. See David T. Canon, *Actors, Athletes, and Astronauts: Political Amateurs in the United States Congress* (Chicago: University of Chicago Press, 1990), 35–37.

122. Dunne, *Monster*, 199.

123. On British cinema's organizational backwardness, see Porter, *On Cinema*, 68–71; and Chanan, "The Emergence of an Industry."

124. The quotation is from Miller's essay, "1956 and All This" (1956), reprinted in Martin and Centola, eds., *Theater Essays of Arthur Miller*, 89. Also relevant are the essays "Tragedy and the Common Man" (1949), 3–7, "The American Theater" (1955), 31–50, and "The American Writer: The American Theater" (1982), 368–83.

125. I am paraphrasing Ethan Mordden, *The American Theatre* (New York: Oxford University Press, 1981), 297–304.

126. Brustein's aspersions appear in "Acting in England and America" (1973), from his book, *The Culture Watch: Essays on Theatre and Society, 1969–1974* (New York: Knopf, 1975), 84–89 (quotations from 85).

127. Rousseau, "Letter to M. D'Alembert on the Theatre," in *Politics and the Arts*, 79.

128. On Forrest, Macready, and the Astor Place Riot, see Bruce A. McConachie, *Melodramatic Formations: American Theater and Society, 1820–1870* (Iowa City: University of Iowa Press, 1992), 65–155; and Lawrence W. Levine,

*Highbrow/Lowbrow: The Emergence of Cultural Hierarchy in America* (Cambridge: Harvard University Press, 1988), 63–69.

129. Erwin Panofsky, "Style and Medium in Motion Pictures" (1934; rev. 1947), in Mast, Cohen, and Braudy, eds., *Film Theory and Criticism*, 233–48.

130. *Macready's Reminiscences, and Selections from his Diaries and Letters* (1875) is excerpted in Cole and Chinoy, eds., *Actors on Acting*, 334–37 (quotation from 335).

131. The idea has been proposed by Joel Porte in his *In Respect to Egotism: Studies in American Romantic Writing* (Cambridge: Cambridge University Press, 1991), 201–206.

132. McConachie, *Melodramatic Formations*, 117.

133. Classic studies of the cinema's naturalism include Kracauer, *Theory of Film*, and Bazin, *What Is Cinema?* The Edison ad, dated 1898–99, appears in Bordwell, Staiger, and Thompson, *The Classical Hollywood Cinema*, 100.

134. See Hansen's brilliant *Babel and Babylon: Spectatorship in American Silent Film* (Cambridge: Harvard University Press, 1991).

135. See Carrière, *The Secret Language of Film*, 86, for the French phrase. He also cites, "Il fait son cinéma," meaning "He's feeding you a line."

136. Griffith is quoted as the epigraph to chapter 3 of Kracauer's *Theory of Film*, 45 (note that "The Redemption of Physical Reality" is Kracauer's subtitle). For Carrière, see *The Secret Language of Film*, 220.

137. See Umberto Eco, *Travels in Hyperreality*, trans. William Weaver (New York: Harcourt Brace, 1986), 7.

138. See Keith Thomas, *Man and the Natural World: Changing Attitudes in England, 1500–1800* (1983; rpt., New York: Oxford University Press, 1996).

139. Quotations are from the edition of *Maggie* reprinted in *The Portable Stephen Crane*, ed. Joseph Katz (New York: Viking, 1969), 34. Additional citations are included in the text.

140. See R. W. Stallman and E. R. Hagemann, eds., *The War Dispatches of Stephen Crane* (New York: New York University Press, 1964), 107–111, 241–44.

141. Richard Chase, *The American Novel and Its Tradition* (New York: Anchor, 1957), 1–28 (James and Melville quoted on 25).

142. James quoted in Chase, *The American Novel and Its Tradition*, 27.

143. From a magazine article in the 1920s, quoted in Emily S. Rosenberg, *Spreading the American Dream: American Economic and Cultural Expansion, 1890–1945* (New York: Hill and Wang, 1982), 103.

144. The numbers are in Giannetti and Eyman, *Flashback*, 521–22; Benjamin R. Barber, *Jihad vs. McWorld* (New York: Times Books, 1995), 92–95; and, for the individual countries, Peter Cowie, ed., *Variety International Film Guide 1997* (London: André Deutsch, 1997).

145. A panic-striken warning can be found in Carrière, *The Secret Langage of Film*, 192–97.

146. See Marcia Landy, *British Genres: Cinema and Society, 1930–1960* (Princeton: Princeton University Press, 1991), 24. Many of the British firms responsible for the "quota quickies" were partly owned by Hollywood studios.

147. For the Marshall Plan conditions of aid, see Reinhold Wagnleitner, *Coca-Colonization and the Cold War: The Cultural Mission of the United States in Austria after the Second World War*, trans. Diana M. Wolf (Chapel Hill: University of North Carolina Press, 1994), esp. 222–74. Wagnleitner, an admirer of American mass culture, speaks of the "Washington-Hollywood axis" (241).

148. For the Farren episode, see McConachie, *Melodramatic Formations*, 144–52.

149. See Michael R. Booth, *Theatre in the Victorian Age* (Cambridge: Cambridge University Press, 1991), esp. 58–59, 71. The quotations are from H. A. Saintsbury and Percy Fitzgerald. Booth's book is also a source for the next three paragraphs.

150. Simon Trussler, *The Cambridge Illustrated History of British Theatre* (Cambridge: Cambridge University Press, 1994), 234.

151. The "photographic ideal" is discussed at length by A. Nicholas Vardac, *Stage to Screen: Theatrical Origins of Early Film—David Garrick to D. W. Griffith* (1949; rpt., New York: De Capo Press, 1987).

152. Booth, *Theatre in the Victorian Age*, 71.

153. This is Levine's thesis in *Highbrow/Lowbrow*.

154. See Richard Shannon, *The Crisis of Imperialism, 1865–1915* (London: Paladin, 1976).

155. On this point, the work of Homi K. Bhabha is highly suggestive. A good introduction is his essay, "Signs Taken for Wonders: Questions of Ambivalence and Authority Under a Tree Outside Delhi, May 1817," in Henry Louis Gates, Jr., ed., *"Race," Writing, and Difference* (Chicago: University of Chicago Press, 1986), 163–84.

156. On working-class acceptance of imperialism, see Gareth Stedman Jones, "Working-class Culture and Working-class Politics in London, 1870–1900: Notes on the Remaking of a Working Class," in his *Languages of Class: Studies in English Working-Class History, 1832–1982* (Cambridge: Cambridge University Press, 1983), 179–238; the quoted phrase is from 181.

157. See Hansen, *Babel and Babylon*, 59–125; also relevant is Robert Sklar, *Movie-Made America*, esp. 3–32.

158. See Walter LaFeber, *The American Age: United States Foreign Policy at Home and Abroad Since 1750* (New York: Norton, 1989); Roosevelt is quoted on 225.

159. See LaFeber, *The American Age*, 213, 222.

160. Michael Paul Rogin observes of *Birth*: "American movies were born . . . in a racist epic." See Rogin's *Ronald Reagan, the Movie, and Other Episodes in Political Demonology* (Berkeley and Los Angeles: University of California Press,

1987), 191. For another perspective on imperialism and early American film, see Slotkin, *Gunfighter Nation*, 231–54. Also relevant are various essays in Amy Kaplan and Donald E. Pease, eds., *Cultures of United States Imperialism* (Durham, N.C.: Duke University Press, 1993).

161. I have relied on two sources for my discussion of the palaces: David Naylor, *American Picture Palaces: The Architecture of Fantasy* (New York: Van Nostrand Reinhold, 1981); and Douglas Gomery, "If You've Seen One, You've Seen the Mall," in Miller, ed., *Seeing Through Movies*, 49–80.

162. Another factor here was the contemporaneous cult of "antimodernism," which stoked fascination with the primitive and exotic. As T. J. Jackson Lears points out in the best study of this phenomenon, antimodernism was clearly linked to the ideology of imperialism. See his book *No Place of Grace: Antimodernism and the Transformation of American Culture, 1880–1920* (New York: Pantheon, 1981).

163. See Hansen's discussion of cinematic universalism in *Babel and Babylon*, 76–80. Dixon is quoted in Raymond A. Cook, *Thomas Dixon* (New York: Twayne, 1974), 121.

164. For the fate of Pathé, see Richard Abel, "The Perils of Pathé, or the Americanization of the American Cinema," in Charney and Schwartz, eds., *Cinema and the Invention of Modern Life*, 183–223. Carrière remarks of cinematic universalism, "It is a language not every people gets to speak. Or more accurately, has the means to speak" (*The Secret Language of Film*, 196).

165. By John Dizikes in his *Opera in America: A Cultural History* (New Haven: Yale University Press, 1993), 502–509.

166. See Belton's *Widescreen Cinema* (Cambridge: Harvard University Presss, 1992). This study is invaluable for details about wide film.

167. For a good brief summary of these events, see Hugh Brogan, *The Penguin History of the United States of America* (1985; rpt., New York: Penguin, 1992), 602–33.

168. See Belton, *Widescreen Cinema*, 99–101, 165.

169. *New York Times*, July 6, 1955, cited in ibid., 90.

170. For a treatment of the plays, see Heidi J. Holder, "Melodrama, Realism and Empire on the British Stage," in J. S. Bratton et al., eds., *Acts of Supremacy: The British Empire and the Stage, 1790–1930* (Manchester: Manchester University Press, 1991), 129–49. Also see Edward W. Said, *Orientalism* (New York: Vintage, 1979).

171. See David Mayer, ed., *Playing Out the Empire: "Ben-Hur" and Other Toga Plays and Films, 1883–1908. A Critical Anthology* (Oxford: Oxford University Press, 1994), esp. Mayer's introduction, 1–20.

172. On religion in the Cold War, see Stephen J. Whitfield, *The Culture of the Cold War* (1991; 2d ed., Baltimore: Johns Hopkins University Press, 1996), esp. 77–100 (Graham is quoted on 81).

173. Nora Sayre analyzes the religious pictures in *Running Time: Films of the*

*Cold War* (New York: Dial Press, 1982), 204–14; the De Mille quote appears on 207.

174. Acheson is quoted in Eric F. Goldman, *The Crucial Decade—and After: America, 1945–1960* (1956; rpt., New York: Vintage, 1960), 125. In addition to Goldman, Brogan, and Whitfield, I have consulted Michael Paul Rogin, *The Intellectuals and McCarthy: The Radical Specter* (Cambridge: MIT Press, 1967); and, on the elitism of foreign policy, William Appleman Williams, *The Tragedy of American Diplomacy* (1959; rpt., New York: Dell, 1972).

175. The quotes are from Belton's *Widescreen Cinema*, 189, 195.

176. The prominence of Englishmen in the toga epics was remarked upon long ago by John Osborne. In *Look Back in Anger* (1956), the protagonist Jimmy Porter attacks his wife Alison as "Lady Pusillanimous" and imagines her with her husband Sextus, "on their way to the Games. Poor old Sextus! If he were put into a Hollywood film, he's so unimpressive, they'd make some poor British actor play the part" (New York: Penguin, 1957), 21–22.

177. See Gabler, *An Empire of Their Own*, 369.

178. See Dizikes, *Opera in America*, 502–509.

179. The importance of music in Brecht is discussed by John Willett, "Ups and Downs of British Brecht," in Pia Kleber and Colin Visser, eds., *Re-interpreting Brecht: His Influence on Contemporary Drama and Film* (Cambridge: Cambridge University Press, 1990), 76–89, esp. 85–86.

180. The information on the theater in this and the next paragraph is taken from J. L. Styan, *The English Stage: A History of Drama and Performance* (Cambridge: Cambridge University Press, 1996); Shaw is quoted on 347 and 341. Also relevant is Raymond Williams, "British Film History: New Perspectives," in Curran and Porter, eds., *British Cinema History*, esp. 18–19.

181. On the end of the British Empire, see M. E. Chamberlain, *Decolonization: The Fall of the European Empires* (Oxford: Basil Blackwell, 1985); and V. G. Kiernan, *European Empires from Conquest to Collapse, 1815–1960* (Bungay, Suffolk: Fontana, 1982).

182. Trussler discusses the postwar consensus in *Cambridge Illustrated History of British Theatre*, 300–301.

183. See Lord Keynes, "The Arts Council: Its Policy and Hopes," *The Listener*, 34 (July 12, 1945), 31–2. Keynes's piece is briefly discussed by Ronald Hayman, *British Theatre since 1945: A Reassessment* (Oxford: Oxford University Press, 1979), 131.

184. Robert Hewison so denominates 1956, although he concentrates entirely on Britain. See his *In Anger: British Culture in the Cold War, 1945–60* (New York: Oxford University Press, 1981), 127–28.

185. This information comes from Goldman, *The Crucial Decade—and After*, 298.

186. The statistics are from Barber, *Jihad vs. McWorld*, 76.

187. See Austin, "Home Video," in Balio, ed., *Hollywood in the Age of Television*, 323–25.

188. See Styan, *The English Stage*, 368. Styan's whole discussion of Brecht and Osborne is excellent (396–402).

189. Osborne, *Look Back in Anger*, 63, 17.

190. The phrase appears in Osborne's stage directions, *The Entertainer* (London: Faber and Faber, n.d.), 12.

191. *The Entertainer*, 73, 78, 32, 86, 7.

192. Quoted in Styan, *The English Stage*, 397.

193. *The Entertainer*, 7.

194. Thomas Elsaesser remarks, "Not a counter-Hollywood superseded Hollywood, but a 'new' Hollywood." For information on Brecht and the movies, see Elsaesser's essay, "From Anti-Illusionism to Hyper-Realism: Berthold Brecht and Contemporary Film," in Kleber and Visser, eds., *Re-interpreting Brecht*, 170–85 (the quotation is from 182); and James Roy MacBean, *Film and Revolution* (Bloomington: Indiana University Press, 1975).

195. On this last point, see in particular Kiku Adatto, *Picture Perfect: The Art and Artifice of Public Image Making* (New York: Basic Books, 1993), esp. 93–94, 168.

196. On racial admixture in modern American art, see Ann Douglas, *Terrible Honesty: Mongrel Manhattan in the 1920s* (New York: Farrar, Straus, and Giroux, 1995). Michael Rogin has written about Hollywood's persistent negrophobia in " 'The Sword Became a Flashing Vision': D. W. Griffith's *The Birth of a Nation*," in *Ronald Reagan, the Movie*, 190–235, and in *Blackface, White Noise: Jewish Immigrants in the Hollywood Melting Pot* (Berkeley and Los Angeles: University of California Press, 1996). I am much indebted to both Rogin studies.

197. Wilson quoted in Slotkin, *Gunfighter Nation*, 240.

198. On post-Reconstruction riots and black disenfranchisement, see Nell Painter, *Standing at Armageddon*, esp. 216–30. On the East St. Louis riot and the epidemic of lynching, see James Weldon Johnson's autobiography, *Along This Way* (1933; rpt., New York: Penguin, 1990), 319–30.

199. On Tillman, see Painter, *Standing at Armageddon*, 160–62.

200. Rosebery is quoted in Michael Pickering, "Mock Blacks and Racial Mockery: The 'Nigger' Minstrel and British Imperialism," in J. S. Bratton et al., eds., *Acts of Supremacy*, 190.

201. James Weldon Johnson, *The Autobiography of an Ex-Coloured Man* (1912, 1927; rpt., New York: Vintage, 1989), 163.

202. All page numbers cited in the text are from *The Clansman* (1905; rpt., Lexington: University Press of Kentucky, 1970).

203. Douglass, *Narrative of the Life of Frederick Douglass, an American Slave*, ed. Houston A. Baker (1845; rpt., New York: Penguin, 1986), 47.

204. Robert Roberts, who grew up in an Edwardian slum, reports that illit-

erate moviegoers "would take children along to act as readers. In this capacity I saw my own first film. When picture gave place to print on the screen a muddled Greek chorus of children's voices rose from the benches, piping above the piano music." See Roberts, *The Classic Slum: Salford Life in the First Quarter of the Century* (1971; rpt., Penguin: London, 1990), 176.

205. Books on Griffith as innovative filmmaker are legion. Examples worth consulting are Paul O'Dell, *Griffith and the Rise of Hollywood* (New York: Castle Books, 1970); Richard Schickel, *D. W. Griffith: An American Life* (New York: Simon and Schuster, 1984); Scott Simmon, *The Films of D. W. Griffith*; and Tom Gunning, *D. W. Griffith and the Origins of American Narrative Film*.

206. Eisenstein's dicussion of Griffith and the novel is reprinted as "Dickens, Griffith, and the Film Today" in Mast, Cohen, and Braudy, eds., *Film Theory and Criticism*, 395–402.

207. The announcement is reprinted in Robert M. Henderson, *D. W. Griffith: The Years at Biograph* (New York: Farrar, Straus and Giroux, 1970), opposite p. 113.

208. The Marsh story comes from O'Dell, *Griffith and the Rise of Hollywood*, 16–17.

209. On this point, see Clyde Taylor, "The Re-Birth of the Aesthetic in Cinema," in Daniel Bernardi, ed., *The Birth of Whiteness: Race and the Emergence of U.S. Cinema* (New Brunswick, N.J.: Rutgers University Press, 1996), 15–37. Taylor's essay is a powerful indictment of the racism that informs the Hollywood aesthetic.

210. Griffith quoted in Lary May, *Screening Out the Past: The Birth of Mass Culture and the Motion Picture Industry* (New York: Oxford University Press, 1980), 76. May discusses Griffith's efforts to make film "a sphere of the sublime" (60–95).

211. See Daniel Bernardi, "The Voice of Whiteness: D. W. Griffith's Biograph Films," in Bernardi, ed., *The Birth of Whiteness*, 103–28.

212. Johnson, *The Autobiography of an Ex-Coloured Man*, 87.

213. Booker T. Washington, *Up from Slavery*, ed. William L. Andrews (New York: Norton Critical Edition, 1996), 71–72.

214. Brook Thomas notes the blind spot in Turner's argument in "Turner's 'Frontier Thesis' as a Narrative of Reconstruction," in Robert Newman, ed., *Centuries' Ends, Narrative Means* (Stanford, Calif.: Stanford University Press, 1996), 117–37, esp. 131–33.

215. The quotes come from Thomas Cripps, *Hollywood's High Noon: Moviemaking and Society Before Television* (Baltimore: Johns Hopkins University Press, 1997), 48 (see also 29–30).

216. Paul Scott, *The Day of the Scorpion*, in *The Raj Quartet* (London: Heinemann, 1976), 300. Also see James Morris, *Pax Britannica: The Climax of an Empire* (1968; rpt., London: Penguin, 1979), 131–55.

217. Morris, *Pax Britannica*, 515; also see Thomas R. Metcalf, *Ideologies of*

*the Raj* (Cambridge: Cambridge University Press, 1994), esp. chapter 3, "The Creation of Difference."

218. According to Laura Tabili, the interwar years brought the Empire-wide system of racialized inequality to England. Before this era, "overt mechanisms of racial subordination like those in the colonies were largely absent." See her book, *"We Ask for British Justice": Workers and Racial Difference in Late Imperial Britain* (Ithaca: Cornell University Press, 1994), 4 and passim. Tabili notes (on 178) that black migrants with their children today amount to less than 4 percent of the British population.

219. Scott, *The Day of the Scorpion*, 300.

220. Important studies of this paradox include Edmund S. Morgan, *American Slavery/American Freedom: The Ordeal of Colonial Virginia* (New York: Norton, 1975); David R. Roediger, *The Wages of Whiteness: Race and the Making of the American Working Class* (London: Verso, 1991); and Eric Lott, *Love and Theft: Blackface Minstrelsy and the American Working Class* (New York: Oxford University Press, 1993). The second Whitman remark appears in Lott, 78.

221. For an interesting treatment of the mystique of interchangeability, see Philip Fisher, "Democratic Social Space: Whitman, Melville, and the Promise of American Transparency," *Representations* 24 (Fall 1988): 60–101.

222. For the argument in this paragraph, see Stephen Orgel, *The Illusion of Power: Political Theater in the English Renaissance* (Berkeley and Los Angeles: University of California Press, 1975); King James I is quoted on 42.

223. See Cole and Chinoy, eds., *Actors on Acting*, 335.

224. Shaw (n.d.) quoted in ibid., 375.

225. Cole and Chinoy, eds., *Actors on Acting*: Gielgud (1939), 398, 401; and Brook (1969), 424.

226. Three valuable works on democratic celebrity and the film star, which I have used for this and the next two paragraphs, are Leo Braudy, *The Frenzy of Renown: Fame and Its History* (New York: Oxford University Press, 1986); Richard Dyer, *Stars* (London: British Film Institute, 1979); and Joshua Gamson, *Claims to Fame: Celebrity in Contemporary America* (Berkeley and Los Angeles: University of California Press, 1994). The quotation is from Gamson, 29.

227. Quoted in Cole and Chinoy, eds., *Actors on Acting*: Spolin (1963), 641–42; Beck and Malina (1970), 653, 658.

228. The first black movie star who neither sang nor danced was Sidney Poitier. He rose to fame in the 1960s but fell out of public favor when he took on more militant roles.

229. Robert La Franco, in an article titled "The Top Forty," reports that the highest show business salary in the United States went to Oprah Winfrey for the combined years 1995 and 1996, when she earned $171 million. Michael Jackson was number four on the list and Bill Cosby number 31. The best-paid black film star during the same period was Denzel Washington, who logged in at number

36 with a salary of $30 million. Admittedly, this is a staggering figure, and it may seem strained to speak of Hollywood blacks as still suffering from discrimination. But it should be noticed that fully a dozen white actors came in ahead of Washington, all of them male: Arnold Schwarzenegger at number 7, Jim Carrey at 9, Tom Hanks at 15, Tom Cruise at 17, Harrison Ford at 18, Clint Eastwood at 19, Sylvester Stallone at 21, Robin Williams at 23, Michael Douglas at 26, Bruce Willis at 27, John Travolta at 32, and Kevin Costner at 35. Demi Moore dropped out of the top forty because of the failure of *Striptease* (1996). The only female star to make the list was Sandra Bullock at number 40 (salary: $25 million). La Franco's piece appears in *Forbes* 158 (September 23, 1996): 164–78.

230. On the prehistory of the English national theater, see Loren Kruger, *The National Stage: Theatre and Cultural Legitimation in England, France, and America* (Chicago: University of Chicago Press, 1992), 83–131 (quotation from 99).

231. For voting peculiarities, see Marwick, *British Society Since 1945*, 107.

232. On Blair's adoption of one nationism, see Sidney Blumenthal, "The Next Prime Minister," *The New Yorker* 71 (February 6, 1996): 39–51.

233. Martin Jay summarizes French thought on the movies in his *Downcast Eyes*, 435–91.

234. Cripps's *Hollywood's High Noon* is extremely judicious on film's doubleness, esp. 45–70.

235. David Foster Wallace, *A Supposedly Funny Thing I'll Never Do Again: Essays and Arguments* (Boston: Little, Brown, 1997), 80.

236. For somewhat alarmist accounts of media concentration, see Barber, *Jihad vs. McWorld*, and a special issue of *The Nation* on "The National Entertainment State," 262 (June 3, 1996).

237. See Michael Lind, *Up from Conservatism: Why the Right Is Wrong for America* (New York: Free Press, 1996), 247–50.

238. See Baldwin's *The Devil Finds Work: An Essay* (New York: Dial Press, 1976), 6–7.

239. The quotation is from Cameron's "scriptment" for *Strange Days* (New York: Plume, 1995), 39. Although Cameron usually directs his own scripts, the director of *Strange Days* was Kathryn Bigelow. *Strange Days* may have been partly inspired by an earlier film, the 1990 Carolco production of *Total Recall* (starring Arnold Schwarzenegger and Sharon Stone). In this picture, residents of the future can avoid the hassle of physically vacationing on Mars or Saturn by having memories of extraterrestrial holidays implanted in their brains for a fee.

240. And not just popular culture. David Foster Wallace's postmodern novel, the gargantuan *Infinite Jest*, plays a variation on the idea. An experimental filmmaker named James O. Incandenza commits suicide after having produced a masterwork, the eponymous *Infinite Jest*. The picture literally kills viewers

with pleasure. They get so hooked that they are unable to tear themselves away even to eat or sleep. The notes to Wallace's novel contain a filmography of Incandenza's works, referring to his "radical experiments in viewers' optical perspective and context." See *Infinite Jest* (Boston: Little, Brown, 1996), 993.

241. The passage appears in Booker T. Washington's *Up from Slavery*, 130.

242. See Edward N. Wolff, *Top Heavy: The Increasing Inequality of Wealth in America and What Can Be Done about It* (New York: New Press, 1995), 21–25 and passim (the quotation is from 21).

# Index